I HAD NO IDEA YOU WERE BLACK

Navigating Race on the Road to Leadership

BY RONALD A. CRUTCHER

D0103500

To Betty Joy,
my loving wife, life partner, and friend.

Table of Contents

Author's Note

THIS BOOK IS BASED ON my recollections and perspectives on significant moments in my life. There are a few instances where I have withheld the names of certain individuals to respect their privacy, and while I have a good memory, there may be places where others would dispute the facts. If so, my message endures.

Foreword

IN THIS UNPRECEDENTED HISTORICAL MOMENT, when hope is a word rarely heard and an emotion challenged daily, the time is so right to identify the people who provide it. Indeed, there is hope to be found in our history and in people who have been empowered by it. People like Ronald Crutcher.

For generations here in America, Blacks in particular have faced and overcome challenges that sometimes defy belief. While the familiar saying that "it takes a village to raise a child" originated in Africa, its truth threads through every generation, from the first ones brought to these shores from Africa to how we live today. Indeed, the history of Black people in America is replete with stories not only of survival, but of prosperity, despite centuries of effort to keep us, if not enslaved, subjugated.

I had not met Ronald Crutcher when he invited me to speak at Miami University in Ohio, where, in 2002, he was a professor of music as well as provost and executive vice president for Academic Affairs. But after Googling him, I was so delighted that I travelled from South Africa, where I was based at the time, to Oxford, Ohio, a trip of more than twenty hours. From our very first meeting, there was something about then-Provost Crutcher that resonated deeply within me. But I couldn't put my finger on it. I don't think it was the bow tie he wore, since I am not a big fan of bow ties, except when my husband (also a Ronald) wears one on formal occasions. And while this moment was not a formal occasion, on Ronald Crutcher it seemed to fit perfectly. Not that he was a stiff. Indeed, it was his welcoming, gentle demeanor that immediately took my mind off the bow tie.

In no time, I had put my travel exhaustion on hold and found myself wrapped in the garment of warm welcome generated by the Provost. As the day went on, I was struck by Provost Crutcher's genial openness to all he encountered—whether other faculty members or the students casually assembling in the auditorium for the big event. And yet, I continued to sense something about him that spoke of a bond I could not quite identify. Was it that we shared a connection with Germany? Likely not, as mine was a language course during my freshman year in college, while he had lived there, became fluent, studied cello and musicology, and performed in some of the great halls of Europe.

Sometime after the assembly, in a quieter moment with Ron's highly accomplished wife, Dr. Betty Neal Crutcher,

I learned of still another link: though a few years apart, we shared the same February B'Earthday. How encouraging that was to me! It meant that we swam in the same Pisces waters!

It is hard to pinpoint the genesis of many enduring connections. But those few moments of kinship formed the basis of what has since become an abiding friendship. Ron and I stayed in touch as he moved on to assume the presidency at Wheaton College, and invited me to give the first commencement address of his tenure there. I was a bit daunted by the list of speakers who had preceded me in earlier years. But I so trusted my Pisces-brother president that I put those worries aside and prepared to make yet another twenty hour flight to the U S of A

As our friendship grew, I learned a great deal more about Ron Crutcher's remarkable history, for he is not one to blurt it out, even over a period of years. While we share some experiences of growing up in the segregated South, where authorities tried their best to ensure that we accepted the notion of being inferior, the road Ron travelled was rockier than mine. Yet the similarities resonate. Both of our fathers served with dignity in the United States Army, even while the powers that be didn't recognize them as full citizens of the country they were serving. Both of our mothers refused, each in their own way, to accept society's lie of separate but equal. And when Ron and I made it into previously all-white institutions, both of us endured indignities due to our color.

But those experiences, while painful, fed our determination to keep on keepin' on with a vision that helped us transcend challenging circumstances. Our respective journeys taught us how to reach back into our history and learn, perhaps foremost, how our people made a way out of no way, and whose lessons in dignified endurance informed our journey. These lessons have clearly inspired Ron Crutcher through all of his many incarnations—in academia, music, family life, and as a highly respected citizen of the world. Now, as an author, he bears witness to this history and how to use it in challenging times like these, when division tears at the very seams of our union. Ron's words embrace and encourage the hopeful, as well as the hopeless, providing a roadmap to move us forward with an approach aimed at closing the deep divides in our country. His words and leadership show us that it is possible to bring together people with different points of view, through listening with respect, working toward tolerance, and ultimately, hopefully, finding common ground.

This eloquent book provides a light through the darkness to help us all—regardless of race, creed, or political persuasion—as we navigate the often perilous journey toward a more perfect union.

Charlayne Hunter-Gault
Journalist and Child of the Civil Rights Movement

Prologue

TWENTY-FIVE YEARS AGO, long before I'd become a college president, I was hurrying to meet with the CEO of an oil company to discuss the possibility of his funding a scholarship for violin students. He was the chairman of a foundation that provided financial support for violin study. We'd never met. But I was head of the School of Music at the University of Texas at Austin—not exactly riffraff—and this moment had been months in the making. We said hello, shook hands, and sat down to talk.

"I had no idea you were Black," he said.

I was angry. I took a long breath. This was not at all how I'd imagined our conversation beginning. By this point in my career I was an accomplished cellist and educator who'd toured internationally and earned Yale University's first doctorate in cello performance. But now I wondered if I should just cut the conversation short and walk away. Instead, I decided to listen.

The man continued to talk. He and his wife had attended the Aspen Music Festival for several years, and they rarely saw any string players of color in the orchestra. He wondered aloud about the dearth of string players of color, and whether the classical music community could do better in nurturing artists from varied backgrounds. Here was my opening—after all, I was there on a mission—so I talked about what UT was trying to do in that regard. I told the CEO about one student in particular, a young woman of color in whom I saw enormous potential for a career in classical music. The CEO and I both loved the same art form, I realized, and there we could connect, our shared enthusiasm for classical music overshadowing my initial discomfort. A few weeks later, the music school had its scholarship. And my student went on to earn a coveted position in the viola section of the Cleveland Orchestra.

I tell this story often as a lesson of sorts. But over the years, students' reactions to it have changed. These days, their primary response is horror at what they see as the CEO's unpardonable insensitivity around race. *What specifically do you find offensive?* I ask those who talk with me in my current office at the University of Richmond. *How would you have responded? How could the CEO have initiated this conversation in manner less offensive to you?* There is no right answer, of course. My sole aim is to spur their thinking, to continue the conversation.

But that has become an increasingly difficult job.

While universities have traditionally served as safe zones for pondering such questions, the politics and rhetoric now inflaming the nation have spilled over to foment a climate of campus unrest at such a decibel level that even the most innocent inquiry becomes suspect.

To be sure, not all inquiries are innocent. But since 2015, student demonstrations over free speech and racial bias have resulted in faculty firings, resignations, and physical assaults on campuses from Washington State to Connecticut. Warring ideas (rather than actual wars) even resulted in a politically motivated shooting.

At Yale University, a firestorm around the mere suggestion that racially insensitive Halloween costumes could occasion discussion—rather than outright censure—forced the termination of one professor. The student who'd led the charge was later honored with an award for fostering interracial understanding.

At the Evergreen State College in Washington, a teacher who'd questioned an equity policy that asked white students to leave campus for a day and reflect on their racial privilege was hounded by a crowd that gathered outside his classroom, shouting, chanting, and demanding his resignation. They were successful. But the threat of violence in response became credible enough that Evergreen's leaders eventually decided to hold graduation off campus.

In this swirling cauldron of overheated rhetoric, I invited former Bush Administration advisor Karl Rove, one of the most polarizing political figures of the past two decades, to sit with me on a dais at the University of Richmond and discuss immigration policy. I'd been prepared for an outcry, and we had plainclothes security details stationed all over campus. Yet there were no outbursts.

Earlier in the day Rove had spoken to a class on leadership, where students vigorously challenged his opinions on gun control and the Iraq War. After the talk on immigration, he appeared at a public reception—laughing, chatting, standing for photos.

Several months later, when anti-LGBTQ writer Ryan Anderson came to campus at the invitation of a conservative student group from our law school, some faculty objected, stating that Anderson's views were "transphobic." Several LBGTQ students echoed those concerns. But I insisted that we allow him to talk. This was an opportunity for discussion and debate, I felt. I hoped it might nudge students disgusted with Anderson's positions to marshal arguments proving him wrong. Anyone with a voice can shut down speakers, but meaningful understanding grows every time we open ourselves to someone who is different from us, whether in background or beliefs— rather than retreating into censorship motivated by fear.

Do not misunderstand: there is much about the current tenor of rhetoric in this country that offends me. The racially charged riots in Charlottesville—just an hour's drive from my own campus—were a wake-up call to the true tenor of white supremacy in America. But I believe we grow when listening to views that differ from our own, even when they anger us. This is much easier said than done. Listening requires patience, discipline, empathy, and intellect—the building blocks of civility.

This insistence on listening—essential for any musician, of course—has informed my approach to leadership ever since I entered higher education administration in 1988, at the University of North Carolina. It requires that I silence gut reactions and think before speaking. It has also allowed me a hand in shaping the education of thousands of young people.

Yet if not for an unexpected conversation one day in 1997, I might never have ascended to this position. By then, I was running the School of Music at the University of Texas at Austin—the same place where my Blackness had shocked the oil company CEO—and a musician I'd long revered invited me to lunch. We all have our icons, and Bryce Jordan—a flutist and musicologist who'd become the first musician appointed president of a large university—was one of mine. Jordan had had much to do with convincing me to move my family to Texas in the first place, and I considered him a mentor. But I expected our meeting on this day to be all business.

I rode an elevator up to the Headliners Club restaurant, on the top floor of the Chase Tower in Austin, thinking about UT-Austin's upcoming capital campaign and the funding priorities that I wanted to discuss with Jordan. But as we began to eat, he launched into his larger agenda. "It's obvious to me that you're going to be a college president," he said. "Have you thought about what kind of school you'd like to lead?"

I was caught completely off guard. In quiet moments I'd considered the idea of a college presidency, but it was more of a fantasy—nothing I ever said out loud or pondered in any depth. So, I panicked. This was my mentor, after all, a man I'd looked up to for decades, and I had no idea how to answer his question. I tried to sound cool.

"Well, probably no place as big as UT. I don't know, maybe a small liberal arts college?" I said affecting an off-hand manner.

This seemed to satisfy Jordan. But throughout the rest of the lunch I was distracted—tormented, even—by the question and my unconsidered response. Afterward, I wandered, racking my brains—what should I have said, and why had I answered the way I did? What did I even know about small liberal arts colleges? I walked into the campus bookstore and made straight for the college admission section, the shelves with all those heavy reference books listing schools around the country. And there it was, right in front of me: *Colleges That Change Lives* by Lauren Pope.

I flipped to the introduction and my eyes caught on one phrase: "...these are colleges that transform the lives of the students who attend them," it said. In that moment, I knew. This would be my life's work, the goal shaping every decision going forward from that moment. I wanted to lead a school that changed lives.

Seven years later I was named to my first presidency, at Wheaton College in Norton, Massachusetts, which was nearly all white when I showed up. There, too, I heard comments that might have knocked me off balance. "They want to interview you again," the executive search consultant told me after I'd become a finalist. "They feel that you're like Teflon. They don't believe a Black man could be so unimpeachable. You just seem too perfect."

Prologue

I'd long since learned to hush my gut response to such comments, to understand that they sometimes came across in unintended ways. Had I grown angry at the CEO who blurted his ignorance about classical musicians of color, I might never have made it to the lunch with Bryce Jordan. And if I'd never pursued that unexpected conversation about ambition, I might not have found my life's work. This book is the story of how I built my particular brand of leadership, one focused on bridging divides in race, class, and politics through higher education.

Chapter One:
THE DIFFICULTY OF DIVERSITY

IN THE SPRING of 2020, I stood on a stage in Washington, DC, and talked for a good forty-five minutes about transforming the University of Richmond into a high-functioning culture of true inclusivity. Before me and my colleagues sat about one hundred academics and thinkers, all assembled for the annual meeting of the Association of American Colleges and Universities. The applause was enthusiastic, and I was proud of it. I'd come to Richmond with big ideas on this topic, honed over a lifetime of navigating race in higher education, and I'd been glad to report significant progress to the dignitaries seated before me. The very next day, a Black student on my campus discovered the N-word scrawled outside her residence hall door. Another student, from Pakistan, had found "PAKI" written on hers. And a third student, from Afghanistan, saw "Terrorist" scrawled on her name tag. A day later, there were two more incidents. One was a brawl between a Chinese student and his roommate, a football player. The other involved three white sorority sisters tearing down a sign advertising our second annual Black Excellence Gala. Unbeknownst to them their actions were captured by a video camera.

One of the main reasons I'd accepted the job as president at Richmond, which sits on almost four hundred acres of a former plantation, was the university's progress with respect to diversity. Under my predecessor, students of color at UR had nearly tripled as a percentage of the population, and the number of low-income students had nearly doubled, with a notable increase among those who were the first in their families to enroll in higher education, as I had been in my own.

I spoke about this during my 2015 inaugural address at Richmond, urging the campus community to be as purposeful about harnessing the power of our diversity as we had been in creating it. My inaugural symposium that weekend, titled "America's Unmet Promise," had focused on equity and access in high-quality education. My idea was to begin a campus-wide conversation.

The truth is, because most neighborhoods in the United States are places of de facto segregation, residential campuses are the most diverse communities that many of our students have ever experienced, and that provides an extraordinary opportunity. Recent research shows that 91% of white people associate only with other whites. It's a similar pattern among Blacks, with 83% maintaining social relationships only with people of their race; Hispanic

Americans are at 64%. Against societal patterns like that, college is one of the best—and perhaps last—opportunities many young people will have to live in community with those who come from worlds different from their own.

I believe in my core that one of the duties of a liberal education is to help young people develop the capacity to interact with others in honest and direct ways. It's good for the intellect, and in my view, it is also essential for a functioning democracy. Hence my focus that fall afternoon when I started at UR. Now, as I spoke in Washington, DC, only five years later, was the bitterest evidence of how far we had yet to go.

In truth, it was not entirely surprising.

Shortly after I'd taken the job and arrived on campus, I requested disaggregated data on outcomes: graduation and retention rates for traditionally disadvantaged groups, as well as indicators of their participation in what I call "high-impact practices"—internships, research, and study abroad—beause I wanted to know if low-income students and students of color were getting the same kind of academic experience as other young people. It is one thing to change your demographics, but that means little if the actual experience of traditionally disadvantaged students falls short.

To my delight, the numbers were great. Across nearly every category, historically underrepresented students were taking advantage of our offerings at rates that matched or exceeded campus averages. The only exception was study abroad: students of color were only half as likely to take classes internationally. So I set about developing a program to bridge that gap. Given these remarkable demographic changes within a rather short period of time and the lack of any significant achievement gaps between UR's various demographic groups, I'd concluded that we had a legitimate opportunity at the University of Richmond to develop a truly skilled intercultural community, a place where all members have the capacity to interact with each other in honest and direct ways across the divides of race, gender, politics, and religion. I hadn't seen many such places, despite much posturing talk from educational leaders.

But the bloom faded fast. Despite the encouraging numbers, I was beginning to see daily evidence that students of color and those from low-income families were not doing so well, after all. One study indicated that many had enrolled at UR because of our generous financial aid, but they weren't actually thriving. Exhibit A: the racist and humiliating smears experienced by three young students at the very moment I was trumpeting Richmond's success in Washington, DC.

Naturally, news of these incidents spread rapidly, igniting outrage across our campus and beyond. The Chinese Students and Scholars Association wrote me to express their shock and dismay. The university's Black Student Alliance, Multicultural Student Solidarity Network, and student government each issued statements saying UR had failed to live up to our mission of ensuring every student was treated as a "valued member of our community."

Parents started calling and emailing with concern about their children's safety on campus, and local media flooded us with inquiries. The Board of Trustees wanted to know how I planned to respond.

For a month, I met regularly with affected groups on UR's campus, so that they could inform our next steps. I made a point of being present at student-led initiatives, from a speak-out on our university forum to a silent protest at a men's basketball game. I established a President's Student Cabinet to ensure that UR's leaders had regular communication with students, and we committed to creating a permanent multicultural space on campus. Ultimately, I hosted a campus-wide community meeting that brought together more than five hundred people to listen to students' experiences and expressions of hurt, anger, and frustration. When a young Black woman told me she had been singled out in class and asked to speak for all Black folks, I was thrown backward into memories of my own childhood and college experiences more than five decades past. It was among the most painful moments I had experienced in my forty-three years in higher education.

Sadly, the perpetrators of these heinous acts were never identified. Had they been, I am certain people would have called for their expulsion. But I would have vigorously resisted that kind of "justice." In my opinion, it would be little more than giving them a free pass to ignore the harm they'd caused and, perhaps, to walk away feeling aggreived. Instead, I would have tried to educate them about the visceral impact of their behavior. If the three victims had been willing, I would have organized a facilitated conversation between them and the perpetrators, then ongoing intergroup dialogs culminating in having each write about what they might have learned. Finally, I would have invited them to my office for a face-to-face conversation about their overall experience. What I am describing here is a deep learning experience—because, after all, we are an educational institution.

In all honesty, I'd expected that America would be past this by now, so far into the twenty-first century. That was my naivete. Racial divides are this country's original sin, the mark that continually prevents us from living up to our founding ideals. My concerns are not merely philosophical. Being able to work across divides is, to my mind, a sign of intellectual strength and maturity, which is what we in higher education are charged with cultivating. The reality is every college president will almost certainly face similar crises, given that social inequities remain pervasive in our country. This book lays out the story of how I learned to navigate them in my own life and the leadership lessons I picked up along the way.

Lesson One: *Acknowledging an uncomfortable history can lead to conversations that point the way forward.*

In addition to my US education career, I've spent considerable time living in Germany as a classical cellist. This has provided an interesting vantage point from which to view race in America, and to compare the ways another country handled its own ugly past. On the sidewalks of many towns and cities in Germany, for instance, are installations of *Stolpersteine*, or stumbling stones. These concrete cubes, each bearing a brass plate inscribed with the names and fates of Holocaust victims, provide a subtle yet consistent reminder that physically forces pedestrians to remember the past.

I believe this kind of engagement is essential, and as a nation the US has so far avoided it, never fully grappling with the psychological and economic aftermath of slavery, segregation, lynching, and ongoing systemic disparities. But it may surprise readers to learn that on the UR campus, I am not seen as a standard-bearer of progressivism or political correctness.

Since 2016, I have become increasingly concerned about the lack of thoughtfulness, integrity, and empathy in America's public discourse. Though the strength of democracy depends upon the ability to have robust discussions—even disagreements—without acrimony, young people have few role models in this regard. On campus, we've attempted to model thoughtful dialog through a lecture series aptly titled Sharp Viewpoints, which is designed to present competing perspectives on topics crucial to our nation. But my choice of speakers for the series—including Karl Rove on immigration and Jonathan Haidt on *The Coddling of the American Mind*—has often run afoul of our progressive faculty. The lecture series during 2020 focused on the health of our democracy. The objective was to model how thought leaders from opposite sides of a political divide could nonetheless engage in a civil, substantive conversation about the most pressing and polarizing issues of our time. Generally, we did better than speakers on the national stage.

Lesson Two: *Respond to controversial speech with more speech.*

During the fall of 2018, when a conservative student organization from the University of Richmond School of Law invited Ryan T. Anderson, of the Heritage Foundation, to speak on campus, many people called for me to disinvite him. Anderson's views were transphobic, they alleged. Some LBGTQ students and employees said his presence on campus made them feel unsafe.

I empathized. As a Black man in America, I know well the discomfort and, at times, fear that can come from the words of others. Yet, while I strongly support transgender rights and disagree strongly with Anderson's beliefs, I insisted that we allow him to speak. Anderson's thinking was influencing decision-makers and had been cited in two Supreme Court cases. As several professors pointed out, their students needed to be familiar with the case law Anderson would be referencing—whether or not they agreed with it. Moreover, one of our law professors would be providing a rebuttal following Anderson's remarks. In my mind, the talk would be a valuable educational opportunity for our students to see how one can hold speakers accountable for their words and, if they so choose, how to protest peacefully. Indeed, I believe we have a responsibility as educators to help students craft counter-arguments and develop the intellectual strength necessary to rebut perspectives they find personally challenging. In my opinion, we do not help them develop those muscles by insulating them from speakers who offend.

Ultimately, Dr. Anderson came to campus, and members of our community protested his appearance vigorously, but peacefully. Students dressed in white stood in silence, one by one, holding signs of protest. After Anderson's remarks, law professor Jud Campbell joined him on stage for a spirited debate, demonstrating how to marshal arguments against someone with whom you disagree. A group of law students lined up during the question and answer period to pose pointed queries. Later, one of the protesters who identified as transgender engaged Anderson in a one-on-one conversation and reflected on the experience in our student newspaper: "Coming into this was really hard for me because it's really easy to vilify someone when you haven't met them," they wrote. "It's hard to hate someone when you meet them."

I'll go out on a limb and suggest that this meeting between a young adult and someone they perceived as an enemy was among the most valuable educational experiences that student had all year. The exchange exemplified my firmly held belief that our campuses can serve as laboratories for democracy.

But not if debate and dissention are silenced.

Lesson Three: *Slow down.*

At the University of Richmond, our student government passed a resolution in 2019 demanding that we remove the name of Robert Ryland, the university's first president—and a slave owner—from our oldest campus building. We took this as an opportunity to educate them on our full history. Many students were surprised to learn that Ryland was not only a Baptist minister implicated in slavery, but also a man who taught his worshipers at the African Baptist Church to read and write at a time when it was against the law. I should note that the Rylands are also valued members of our university community today, and it is important to us as an institution to give them time and space to share their perspectives, too.

Diversity is not beneficial if it is merely ceremonial. If various groups do not interact substantively, what is the point? In my opinion, one of the reasons that diversity has been misunderstood, and sometimes maligned, is that people perceive it primarily as a social justice corrective to help "other folks" gain opportunity. While this is part of it, and certainly worthy, we as leaders must do better at making the case for diversity as a benefit to everyone.

From my own experiences of marching in the aftermath of Dr. Martin Luther King Jr.'s assassination to serving as a conscientious objector to the Vietnam War, I have come to believe that free speech is the single greatest tool we have to fight for a more just and equal society. Given the era of renewed civil rights activism in which the US finds itself today, one might expect a certain kinship between current college students and those of us who were on the front lines of protest in the 1960s. But today's young intellectuals are likely to believe that free speech *conflicts* with inclusion—to the degree that they will try to quash debate when a controversial speaker comes to campus, as happened to Charles Murray at Middlebury in 2017. In today's "cancel culture," marked by an absence of intellectual humility and the capacity to forgive, true diversity turns out to be extremely difficult. No wonder 80% of those surveyed by the think tank and research group More in Common said "political correctness is a problem in our country."

The Civil Rights generation in which I came of age did not honestly confront just how difficult true diversity would be. We made it sound as if all that was required was being "open" to people different from ourselves, when the fact is, real inclusivity can be awkward and uncomfortable. It is not simply about linking arms and singing "Kumbaya"!

It takes work, in other words, emotional sweat. Students must be intentional about seeking out friends, classmates, and mentors from different backgrounds and cultures. For those new to campus, this is particularly difficult because they already feel unsure and it feels easier to acclimate around people whose slang and codes of behavior they already understand. Comfortable as this kind of sorting may be, it is antithetical to the spirit of democracy, whose lifeblood is the energetic exchange of diverse and competing ideas.

For these reasons, I make a point of prodding students about their social networks. Do they consist of people from various backgrounds and academic disciplines, or are they filled only with people of the same beliefs? If the latter, I challenge them to reach out to a classmate who is different—whether culturally, politically, or religiously—and get to know them by asking questions and listening, really listening, to the response. The purpose is not to hone debate skills, nor to lay blame; such approaches change nothing. And we are a society in dire need of change.

In fact, I believe we are at an inflection point in US history. The protests against police brutality sparked by the horrific murder of George Floyd brought me to tears and forced me to confront ghosts I thought I'd long ago laid to rest. Walking down Richmond's Monument Avenue, a promenade until recently lined with statues of Confederate heroes Robert E. Lee, Stonewall Jackson, Jefferson Davis, and J. E. B. Stuart, I now feel tremendous conflict. Almost all of them have now been removed—some toppled by protesters—and Lee's removal has been ordered by Virginia Governor Ralph Northam (though at this writing that is still being argued in court). I applaud the governor for taking that bold action against a monument to racism. And I believe the graffiti covering Lee's pedestal tells an important story that should be memorialized. But I can't help feeling perplexed by what cropped up in its place—people barbequing and blasting music throughout the night, driven by a free-floating rage that seems to be building toward—what? No goal I can see, other than vague demands to "defund the police."

To be sure, major changes to our social and economic infrastructure are necessary to eradicate injustice and implement systemic change. In my opinion that is best achieved through coalitions of people working together. Yes, widespread demonstrations during the summer of 2020 got people's attention. But to achieve sustained change we cannot just burn it all down. Social justice groups will need to work effectively with government, business, religious, and community leaders. And that means learning how to work across divides.

UR's goal of becoming a skilled intercultural community does not mean that we expect to become a utopia, immune from racist or xenophobic incidents. The goal is merely to ensure that we have the capability, as a community, to deal with social disruption.

So now, when talking with students, I urge them to strive toward a deeper understanding of why individuals with different views think and believe as they do. These conversations sometimes lead to bruised feelings. But I tell my mentees that this is exactly how they will develop the energy, civility, and substance to navigate differences with power. In the process, their own beliefs get tested and refined, and that will better prepare them for engaged citizenship. I strongly believe that our entire country could benefit from a similar approach.

Chapter Two:
CAN YOU HEAR ME NOW?

DURING MY LENGTHY academic career, I've witnessed significant disruption and change on college and university campuses, from violent anti-war protests, to the deseg regation of higher education in the South, to affirmative action challenges decided by the US Supreme Court. Throughout all of those battles, one distinguishing fact remained consistent: the arguments were public—exceedingly so. Conversation around divisive issues may have convulsed campuses, but it was robust, even welcomed. Today, we see something completely different: the willingness to exclude—or outright disinvite—speakers who are controversial. It is tearing our campuses apart. Of course, academia has rarely been insulated from changing political winds, certainly not in contemporary America. But during the past five years, my colleagues across the country, from Vermont to Missouri to California, have been blindsided by demonstrations protesting speakers—or faculty—perceived to be inflammatory, bigoted, or even just politically right-leaning. In fact, most college presidents (myself included) have been forced to confront bullies seeking to restrict the intellectual freedoms they claim to cherish.

I'm going to call it like I see it: many of these demonstrations are specifically intended to intimidate, to shame the "other side" into silence. As educators leading institutions dedicated to teaching and learning, our mission is to stand up to this dangerous brand of intellectual dishonesty.

Easier said than done. Many of our faculty and staff have an impulse to "protect" our students from voices that they perceive to be not merely offensive but actually "harmful" to their emotional wellbeing. There is a real cost to this urge to shield. In his 2018 book, *The Coddling of the American Mind*, psychologist Jonathan Haidt, who studies morality, discusses the new culture of "safetyism"—most evident these days through the creation of so-called safe spaces, trigger warnings, and the emergence of a "call-out" culture designed to embarrass those who espouse unpalatable beliefs. That seems a very slippery slope; call-out culture allows students to attack a person who claims she's starving (at worst, an obtuse figure of speech) because, of course, she is not *really* starving! In this climate of "safetyism," it becomes common for students, out of fear of misspeaking, to censor themselves. One of my mentees who happens to be biracial wrote a piece describing his white female classmate who was curious about Ta-Nahesi Coates's life as a Black man. The class was reading Coates's work, and she wanted to delve more deeply into his experience. She stuttered and stammered through a few questions, ultimately silencing herself in order to avoid the possibility of saying anything that might be interpreted as racist or privileged.

This is no way to learn. And, as my mentee rightly pointed out in his op-ed, "Dear fellow Black people," those are restraints never applied to discussions of, say, the Holocaust or anti-Semitism. Such a classroom does nothing to help students develop inner strength, the courage of their convictions, or even the ability to have a frank conversation about a difficult topic.

It's not only going on in classrooms. After the Charlottesville demonstration in August 2017, purportedly a protest against the removal of a statue of Confederate General Robert E. Lee that devolved into an anti-Semitic rally, organized marchers carried torches, shouting, "Jews will not replace us!" One of them killed a young woman by plowing his car into the crowd of counter-demonstrators. A month later, as school was getting started that fall, students on my campus—just an hour away—asked me to moderate a discussion about Charlottesville. The aim was both catharsis and strategy session, because the demonstrators were said to be planning a similar march through Richmond during Parents' Weekend. Our talk took place in a business school lecture hall with seats for about three hundred people. The place was packed. Four professors had been invited to speak as a panel, and one of them, a Black sociology teacher close to my daughter's age, pointed out that virulent racism existed right here on our own University of Richmond campus. She described an incident I'd heard nothing about until that moment: students of color had been "terrorized," she said, by the appearance of a noose hanging in the theatre department the previous year.

No one responded. So, rather reluctantly, I weighed in. It was unfortunate that students had been frightened by this insensitive act, but the noose was just an inanimate object, I said, even if it was aimed to intimidate. I'd always been taught that "sticks and stones may break my bones, but words will never hurt me." This was a provocative thing to say, I admit, but I couldn't help myself. I'd stood there, silently debating whether to speak my mind—*stay quiet, let it go, you are the university president*—but I felt that an alternate perspective needed to be voiced. I was thinking about the ways these students might navigate the world a decade or two from now. As educators, we're preparing citizens for the long term, not just the moment at hand—terrible though this moment may be. What's going to happen if they encounter something similarly objectionable on a job? Will they quit? Curl into a fetal position and hide under a blanket?

The words were barely out of my mouth when I saw the aghast expression on students' faces. I'd really stepped in it. Worse, I'd failed to follow the advice I used to give my own daughter: "Think before you act." I considered the noose evidence, mainly, of juvenile idiocy. But I'm in my seventies and I've attained a certain position, one that is worlds apart from that of the teenagers sitting in front of me, many of them away from home for the first time during a period of enormous fear, violence, and instability. I'd made a mistake responding to their concerns out of my own experience, without considering how it might strike a roomful of young people confronting threats like this for the first time. Certainly, I should have acknowledged their shock. I'd also waved off the concerns of a much younger academic, a woman who had only recently become tenured and was, furthermore, the first generation in her family to reach such a position. Talk about a power differential.

After the panel discussion, I apologized to the sociology professor. I told her I felt like a cretin, and invited her to my office for further discussion. Her feelings were not so easily hurt, she said. But we did meet for a chat several weeks later. She specializes in researching higher education and identifying ways that it can work better for families and students of diverse communities. I pointed out that we are living only two generations removed from legal segregation; from where I sit, it's not surprising that many institutions are still racist. She criticized that attitude the same way a lot of Black people criticized President Obama: Why wasn't he doing more? Why didn't he move faster?

Again, I found it difficult to contain myself as I listened to her. She clearly believed inanimate objects could psychologically harm students of color, whom she repeatedly referred to as "marginalized." I've always had trouble with that term. To me, it suggests a certain passivity or lack of agency, of allowing yourself to feel pushed aside. Due perhaps to my own upbringing, I'd never felt "marginalized"—not even in 1965 when I was one among a handful of Black undergraduates at Miami University. Alienated, absolutely. But never marginalized. This is a difference that matters. If you feel alienated, you have the power to do something about it; you can decide to build relationships with those from whom you feel separate—or not.

"Marginalization" suggests powerlessness, a state of being completely ignored, without any opportunity to change the situation. As educators, shouldn't our primary job be giving students the tools they'll need to process alienating experiences—no matter how painful they may be? I asked the professor. A few months later, she would write a pointed and controversial piece for *Inside Higher Education*, asserting that it was possible to increase the percentage of minority students on a college campus while doing nothing to address a racially hostile climate.

I thought of Barry Greene who, in 1968, became the first Black student to live on the University of Richmond campus. He'd told me that not until he'd applied, been accepted, and even won a scholarship to UR, did the school inform him that he couldn't reside in the dorms. Barry is a quiet guy—certainly not an agitator in any conventional sense—but he began asking questions about this decision. The school reversed itself and granted him a room, interviewing white upperclassmen to find one who might agree to be Barry's roommate. Things got worse from there. UR's fight song at the time was "Dixie" and its mascot, a spider dressed in a Confederate soldier's uniform. In the dining hall, some students moved their trays to other tables when Barry sat down. Even the Black staffers, the janitors and maids and waiters, thought he must be a troublemaker. Same with the professors. When he walked into their classrooms, Barry could see them thinking, "Who is this guy?" But he didn't shrink away. He didn't allow himself to be marginalized. *If they're going to teach the white kids sitting here with me, they're going to have to teach me, too. And I'm going to sit right up front*, he thought. It wasn't that he was consciously waging battle, just that he'd been raised to get an education, and he was going to get it—no matter what.

In the end, people recognized that. They saw who he was. Barry's father was murdered while he was a student at Richmond, but President George Modlin insisted that he finish his studies without worrying about tuition—the school would see that he was covered. So today, when Barry hears students asking for all-Black safe spaces, he wonders—and he worries. To him, overcoming segregation was the defining watershed of his life. Now he sees students all but asking to bring it back.

Listening to the sociology professor in my office and thinking about Barry Greene, I began to wonder about other members of the faculty, and how they might be guiding students—in particular, students of color—to experience our predominantly white campus from the perspective of the marginalized. I wondered if this attitude was contributing to hypersensitivity at perceived slights (so-called "microaggressions") when interacting with people from different backgrounds—no matter how unintentional a remark might be. It felt like continuously assuming bad faith on the part of other young people who, after all, were also at college trying to learn about life. It certainly discouraged giving them the benefit of the doubt. And I couldn't see how that was helpful—to anyone.

Most students, whatever their color or background, come to college with little experience building cross-cultural relationships. In my view, a university campus is the place to start learning how to do it. But how can anyone learn anything if they're afraid of failing, or offending, or asking an insensitive question? Simultaneously, constant vigilance against affront won't give our students of color the inner grounding they'll need to navigate an endlessly complex world.

Another instructive moment on campus involved the appearance I alluded to earlier, when the controversial writer and social commentator Ryan T. Anderson visited campus in the fall of 2018. Anderson's work asserting that many transgendered people have mental health problems had led to his being labeled "transphobic" by some in the LGBTQ community. But the law school's Federalist Society had invited Anderson to campus to discuss his book *When Harry Became Sally: Responding to the Transgender Moment*. The week before his visit, one of our professors posted the following message to the faculty listserv:

Can You Hear Me Now?

Dear colleagues,

I am troubled to learn that a notoriously transphobic speaker (Ryan T. Anderson) has been invited to speak at the law school on Tuesday. Anderson is the author of "When Harry Became Sally: Responding to the Transgender Movement" and a Heritage Foundation fellow.

...

I'm having flashbacks of the PPEL speaker, Elizabeth Harman (Professor of Philosophy at Princeton University), who spoke on the supposed ethics of aborting gay and Black fetuses to spare them a future of homophobic and racist discrimination, respectively.

I cannot respect free speech that is bigotry disguised as science. These intellectuals are debating my right to exist as a queer and transgender person. By inviting these people to speak at my university is to endorse their work questioning my worth as a human being.

In response, the dean of the law school wrote an email explaining UR's policy of allowing student groups to choose their speakers. She noted the plan for a law professor's rebuttal immediately following Anderson's his remarks. Several other professors also weighed in, suggesting that their students needed to be familiar with the case law Anderson would be referencing. Even law students who disputed his ideas requested that Anderson be allowed to speak. Nonetheless, I received numerous requests from our LBGTQ alumni organization and other faculty to cancel the event. In each case, I pointed out that Anderson's visit had no bearing on our commitment to ensure

23

trans students' full participation and inclusion on campus. Maybe I sounded overly legalistic. But I kept trying to underscore that our job as educators was to help young people develop the internal and intellectual strength necessary to weather perspectives they found personally challenging. I truly believed this moment offered an important lesson, and that our students would come out of it better equipped to fight for a more inclusive society.

You may be surprised, considering this back story, to hear that the Anderson event went amazingly well. Protesters dressed in white carried placards, but they never interrupted the speaker. The question-and-answer period was cordial, and though the topic of trans identity is among the most hotly debated on college campuses today, our students came away having witnessed—and participated in—a civil discussion about it. They became better informed about the science surrounding gender identity, and more aware of how to discuss such divisive topics in an atmosphere of mutual dignity and respect.

I am not one who posits that there must *always* be compromise. But we know that students learn best when they're challenged to tackle hard questions, and when they're taught to have those conversations in thoughtful ways. In a bitterly polarized time, when any discussion around race, religion, gender, or politics teeters on the edge of diatribe or silence, colleges and universities must graduate students who can find a better way. Higher education is uniquely positioned—indeed, it has an explicit responsibility—to model substantive disagreement and dialog in ways that give students information they can take into the classroom, living room, workplace, and voting booth.

Yes, the current political climate is ugly. Yes, we all have opinions about who is right, and who is wrong. The question is, how can we use our nation's growing diversity as a teaching tool to find common ground, respect the backgrounds that lead to different perspectives, and foster meaningful conversations across barriers?

Colleges and universities provide an optimal space to test these rough waters, but not if every day is smooth sailing. The world our students will enter after graduation is riven with difficult discussions and peopled by those with whom they will disagree. As campus leaders, we have a duty to lead by example and prepare our students, not isolate them like hothouse flowers.

For this reason, I've made a point of welcoming guests to the University of Richmond who espouse a variety of ideological perspectives—ushering them through the front door, so to speak. We must fearlessly defend their right to be there, celebrate the debate, prepare to be surprised, and trust that the risk is worth it.

I am no Pollyanna. Given recent public turmoil over guests invited to speak at Middlebury College, where conservative speaker Charles Murray and the faculty member interviewing him were assaulted, and at the University of Washington where a man protesting conservative firebrand Milo Yiannopoulos was shot, we always prepare a detailed security plan. There are uniformed and plain-clothes police officers present as well as designated space set aside for protesters. At the start of each program we reiterate our belief in the right of free expression, emphasizing that we'll remove anyone who restricts the rights of others to listen and learn. We hold everyone (including the speakers) accountable for their words and actions. Despite the racist incidents I noted earlier in which students of color were targeted, I stand by our general policy of inviting debate and allowing the ideas to be aired that some may find controversial. To date, there have been few protesters at our events, and those who have chosen to demonstrate have followed the university's guidelines.

But, sadly, not all students *want* the opportunity to hear different perspectives. A survey released by the free-speech advocacy group FIRE (Foundation for Individual Rights in Education) in 2017 found that while 93% of students interviewed felt that universities should host a variety of speakers on campus, 69% also believed "a speaker's invitation should be withdrawn if the speaker has made racist or hateful comments." Interestingly, in this report, students who identified as Democratic were nineteen points more likely than their Republican peers to believe some speakers should be disinvited.

That view is shared, apparently, by some of our most learned minds. When I invited Bush Administration advisor Karl Rove to participate in a discussion about immigration in 2017, a sociology professor complained. "Why are we always inviting these conservatives?" he said on a faculty listserv. "People like Rove shouldn't be invited to campus." The last thing I want to do is espouse any particular ideology over another, so we did a fact-check. The count among campus speakers was actually six-to-one, in favor of left-leaning points of view.

I was also surprised and more than a bit troubled to read a 2018 Gallup poll that found 37% of college students believe shouting down speakers is sometimes acceptable. I wish that number was smaller—a lot smaller—because I believe much of the fervor surrounding current First Amendment debates is rooted in our refusal to let people speak, freely and uninterrupted. As Nicholas Kristof of *The New York Times* recently wrote: "Civility is not a sign of weakness, but of civilization."

To me, this suggests a need for deeper education around what our Bill of Rights actually says. Only 46% of students in the FIRE survey understood that hate speech is protected by the First Amendment, and 31% thought that it shouldn't be. Furthermore, we need a lot more discussion about the distinction between hate speech and racism. I believe that there is a difference, but nearly half of the 1,250 students who were surveyed said any discussion using derogatory racial language was tantamount to hate speech. Students were much more willing to listen to statements with which they disagreed (59%) than those they found offensive (35%), hurtful (28%), or racist (21%).

These data should be alarming to us. Not because of the political story they tell, but because of the limitations they suggest on our capacity for robust campus dialog.

To wit: in the Gallup poll, 92% of students said they believed political liberals could "freely and openly" express their views on campus. Only 69% said conservatives enjoyed that right. A sizable majority affirmed that the climate on campuses prevents some people from speaking freely, and that those most likely to be silenced tend to hold politically conservative viewpoints.

We need to use this information, and this moment, to teach—about First Amendment protections, the difference between hate and offensive speech, viewpoint diversity, and the characteristics of legal and civil demonstration.

Meaningful understanding, honed through unexpected or uncomfortable experiences, happens every time we open ourselves to someone who is different, whether in ethnic background, sexual orientation, economic status, religious belief, political affiliation, or social ideology. For that to happen, we must commit to listening, even when what we hear knocks us off-balance. Those conversations may not be easy, but they will be educational.

The University of Richmond is far more diverse as we launch into the third decade of the twenty-first century than ever before, and we are using that breadth in the student population to change campus culture. Yes, there will be inevitable backlash, as the racist incidents I described earlier attest. But we must persevere. We want tomorrow's adults to understand the intellectual benefit of living, learning, and playing in a diverse community—in the literal sense of that word, *diverse*. The social problems America faces are knotty and complex. Addressing them effectively will require more perspectives, not fewer, and university campuses provide an ideal environment to show the leaders of tomorrow how to navigate diversity, rethink a position, or stay up late solving the world's problems emboldened by youth, pizza, and caffeine. There are worse ways to spend an evening.

Indeed, this is the very purpose of higher education: to interrogate truths, support arguments with fact and reason, uncover new knowledge, and create greater understanding. At a moment when people increasingly choose echo chambers over challenging conversations, we have to remind ourselves that higher education's purpose is to examine problems through a wide lens and to question received wisdom. If we hope to strengthen our democracy and prove the value of liberal arts education to a skeptical public, we need to embrace diversity in its truest sense: variety.

That, rather than political correctness or social justice, is why free expression and inclusivity must be core values of the academy in the twenty-first century. For this reason, we must continue to invite speakers who will spur debate. Our goal is neither agreement nor conformity, but the energetic exchange of ideas.

Chapter Three:
THE FOUNDATION OF FAMILY

FIFTY-FIVE YEARS AGO, I moved into Room 227 of Stanton Hall, on the classically collegiate campus of Miami University in Oxford, Ohio. There were about ten thousand students at Miami U in those days, only eighty of whom were Black. Two of us resided in Stanton. I wasn't fazed by being in the minority—not at first. For the previous three years, as a high school student, I'd bused to the campus every Saturday morning to take cello lessons from Professor Liz Potteiger, and I had been anticipating the move away from my parents' home in Cincinnati with great excitement.

Having graduated from a predominantly white high school where I was a popular student leader, I'd assumed that I would feel right at home at college. I'd kept a calendar on the wall next to my bed, marking off the days before my new life would begin. But now, as a full-fledged member of the student body, I was shocked and somewhat dismayed to discover that I did not feel at all comfortable.

For a while, I chalked this up to my general nerdiness. I did not smoke or drink, and tended to avoid parties. But it never really abated. I didn't tell anyone about the alienation I felt, not my parents, or Professor Potteiger, or even the other Black students.

I'd grown up in Cincinnati, Ohio, a border town across the river from slaveholding Kentucky that stood as the gateway to the free North. In the years before the Civil War, Cincinnati had been host to numerous stops along the Underground Railroad, as well as several slave catchers—so the city was, strangely and simultaneously, open to progressive thinking and a stronghold for pro-slavery sentiment.

Neither my mother nor father graduated from high school. They were both born in rural Peytontown, Kentucky. My mother, Burdella, was raised just up the road from Peytontown in Burnamtown, a settlement of six homes built by freed slaves, all of them her relatives. She attended a one-room school for "colored" children, where two teachers educated students from the first through eighth grades until they boarded the bus for segregated Richmond High, about ten miles away.

Although my mother did well enough, she'd never liked school. Today, she might be described as a free spirit. Certainly, she was a nonconformist, a woman who marched to the beat of her own drum. She dropped out at the end of tenth grade and worked as a live-in maid for the Dawes family, of Richmond. Mr. Dawes was a military officer, and when he was transferred to northern

Kentucky in February 1939, he took my mother along. She was fifteen years old.

My father, by contrast, loved school and learning, especially math and science, but as the eldest boy among nine children (five girls and four boys), he never even made it to Richmond High. He had to stay home and work the family tobacco farm. For a long time, I avoided talking or even thinking about my parents' humble beginnings. It embarrassed me. These days, I marvel at the distance from their childhoods to mine, to my daughter's. It's a story that mirrors America's and contains all the possibility and complexity of our country's history around race, as well as the pivotal role of education within that story.

My parents had known each other as children, and my father was smitten early. But they were separated when my mother's family moved into her grandparents' suddenly empty home in Burnamtown. According to family lore, the vacancy was prompted by an offer that Mother's grandfather had received to run his hand-built train at an amusement park, near what is now the Greater Cincinnati International Airport. To get this opportunity, however, Papa Burnam had to sign over the patent for the miniature steam engine that he'd designed and built to the white owner of the park.

As an adolescent, my father would walk from Peytontown up the hill to Burnamtown to spend time with Burdella and her large family. Burdella's father had died when she was eleven, after serving abroad in the Army, where he'd contracted pneumonia in France. According to my ninety-six-year-old Aunt Olivia, their dad could barely walk when he finally returned home on the train. He died two days later. After that, my grandmother, Katie Elizabeth Burnam Miller, went to work for the Works Progress Administration (WPA).

Mama Katie, as she was known to me and her twenty-six other grandchildren, taught quilting through a WPA program, first at Berea College, and then in Richmond. She would stay in Richmond with her sister during the week, hiring a woman to watch her seven children back home in Burnamtown. After two years, my mother and her siblings convinced Mama Katie to let them stay home by themselves. So, in the absence of any adults around during the week, my father, his friends, my mother, and her siblings made candy and played cards late into the evening. Today, neighbors might whisper about this. But in rural Black America of the 1930s, it was not unusual.

Great grandparents' 50th anniversary January 30, 1940

Dad really missed Burdella after she and the family for whom she worked moved to Cincinnati in 1939. He saved up his money, and shortly after his eighteenth birthday was riding on a train north to find her. He arrived with less than three dollars in his pocket, and walked the ten miles from Cincinnati Union Terminal to my Great Aunt Helena's home on Ninth Street in the West End, where my mother spent weekends. Aunt Helena gave dad the money to take a bus to Madisonville, a Cincinnati suburb, where he would live with yet another relation, returning to Aunt Helena's home every weekend to visit the woman who would become my mother.

But Burdella did not make it easy for my dad. According to Aunt Olivia, my mother would sometimes excuse herself when dad visited, pretending to go to the bathroom and leaving him just sitting there, while she slipped out the back to go to the movies with her friends. Dad was not deterred; he continued to visit mother each and every weekend. All week long he worked as a chipper in the foundry at the Cincinnati Milling Machine (later the Cincinnati Milacron), the world's largest machine tool company.

Mother and Dad were married on October 14, 1942. The next day, Dad was recruited into the army. He had gone to the Marimont registration site for a deferral, citing his munitions-building at the Milling Machine. Instead, he ended up registered as a private. I'll never know if this was an accident or done on purpose. But the photo taken of my parents shortly after their marriage, with my mother in a dark suit and perfectly coifed hair, my father looking very proud in his army uniform, remains one of my treasured possessions.

Mother and Dad, 1942

By the end of October, dad was on his way to the South Pacific, to serve as a cook and in the motor corps, driving dead bodies through the jungles of the Philippines. He returned home three years later, on December 24, 1945, his pockets full of foreign bills, coins, and souvenirs from his travels. He and mother wasted no time in starting a family. I was born in February, 1947, and my brother Larry eleven months later, in January, 1948. Our younger brother, Gregory, was born several years later, in April, 1955.

Ambitious and a natural leader, Dad went back to the Milacron after he returned from the army, and he remained there for forty-two years, working his way up to become the firm's first Black manager in the mid 1960s.

While Dad served in the military, Mother lived in the Laurel Homes in the West End of Cincinnati, surrounded by her relatives and friends from Kentucky. Shortly after I was born, we moved to the second floor of a two-family home on Eleanor Place in Mount Auburn. This was a working-class neighborhood of small bungalows with manicured yards, and family was never far away. Our new home was owned by a friend of my Aunt Helena, who lived just around the corner; one house from Aunt Helena lived my Aunt Eva Nettie Fife and Uncle Lonnie. Ours was a small apartment, just three or four rooms, and my parents placed the beds for my brother Larry and me in the front. After Larry was born, our mother—who had worked at my Great Aunt Helena's beauty salon—stayed home (occasionally working for my Great Aunt Eva's catering service).

In 1950, my parents purchased the house in which I grew up, a modest, single-family home on Harvey Avenue, in Avondale, one of Cincinnati's first suburbs. We were the second Black family on the street. Our neighbors were primarily Jewish widows, but these differences never dissuaded my father from interacting with anyone he met. Eventually, he became active in the neighborhood association. Even as a newcomer, he was never afraid to speak up. "Wherever you go, don't just stand around with the Black people," he'd tell me when I was a bit older. "Get to know everyone in the room." His rough, often-bombastic style would become a bitter wedge between us as

I grew older. But as I have noted, one of the bedrock concepts of a liberal arts education is the value of stretching intellectually, reaching beyond the place where one began. In his own way, my father taught us the same lesson.

I loved our new house. On move-in day, I kept running upstairs to gape at the bedrooms. For many years, I thought the bed and dresser set I'd discovered in one of them had been left there for us by the former residents, and that this was just another sign of our great fortune in this new home. (Only many years later did I learn that my parents had purchased it and had it delivered.) Shortly after we moved in, my mother went to work at Cincinnati General Hospital, and my brother and I were sent back to the family compound in Peytontown, Kentucky, to live temporarily with our grandmother, Mama Katie.

Country life for two small boys was an adventure. We spent hours fishing and frog hunting at the pond, bringing our catch home for Mama Katie to cook. But these were chaotic years. Larry and I were crammed into a small room next door to our three teenaged uncles. They had to walk through our room and literally climb over us each morning to get downstairs for school. Within two years, we were back home, now living during the week with a woman known to us as Mother Gay. Once, another of Mother Gay's charges goaded me into pulling a fire alarm because I didn't really believe that it would make engines come. "Try it," he dared me.

A few days later, I was face-to-face with a juvenile court judge and had earned my first headline: "Bad boy, Ronald Crutcher, rings false alarm." After a few more mishaps, my mother quit work and brought us home for good.

I often think back to that label, "bad boy," and wonder what might have happened if I'd believed it. Or if the judge decided I had no promise, no hope of a productive future. Or if I hadn't been surrounded by a deeply loving family of people who saw my actions as those of a curious, misguided child—rather than a thug-in-the-making. It is entirely possible, for instance, that had any of these factors been different, I might have acted out in ways that would have hindered my development. My teachers (almost all of whom were white) might then have responded to me as a problem child, rather than seeing who I really was, a very hard-working, well-mannered Black boy.

Ron, 1953

The first week in my neighborhood school was chaotic in an entirely different way. I was assigned to one homeroom, then another, and finally a third. When I asked my mother why, she said, "Because you are very smart, and they want to put you in a class with other smart children."

That got my attention.

South Avondale Elementary grouped students based on intellectual ability, a practice known today as tracking. It is considered somewhat controversial—mainly because Black and brown children are overwhelmingly excluded—but it had its benefits. While other children were drilled on spelling, we learned Italian and French. While other kids were learning by rote memorization, we got privileges like trips to the local television station, where we produced programs and commercials. I remained with this cohort of children through the sixth grade, and while all of us shared academic aptitude, our economic, racial, and ethnic backgrounds were quite varied. My two closest friends in those days were Steven Reece, who was African-American, and Leon Friedberg, who was Jewish.

One of the first purchases my parents made for our new home was a huge console with a radio and record player. Despite their modest means, music was a constant presence in our home. My father, who sang in a semi-professional men's group called the Excelsior Singers, might have become a professional musician if he'd had the opportunity. He had an enormous collection of jazz records, which he played daily in our living room, and my mother developed a lifelong love of opera after listening to live broadcasts on the radio every Saturday afternoon. This love of opera and classical music was in turn passed down to me. I listened to the Beethoven symphonies on a set of vinyl records given to me by my Uncle John Ogletree, who taught piano at one of the local Black churches. The first live performance I ever attended was a children's concert produced by the Cincinnati Symphony, and our neighbors were part of the String Quartet-in-Residence at the University of Cincinnati. In other words, music was everywhere in my young life—so much so that I did not realize this was unusual until many years later.

But what got my dad going even more than jazz was his ham radio, on which he would talk for hours to people from around the world—the Philippines, Japan, Australia, England, and Holland. This fascinated me, though the conversations were pretty generic.

Not so, my father's parenting style. He was strict, regimenting every hour of the week, and easily angered—especially when he came home from work. He tended to bark orders. For years I thought I hated him. But the fact is, I was ashamed of the way he spoke, so crass and loud, the way he flicked the lights on and off to wake us up for church, the way he had so little education. Whenever he spoke, I pretended that whatever book I was reading was far more interesting, as if I couldn't be bothered to listen.

Many years later, when I was an adult with a child of my own, my father apologized for his hard ways. He'd been taught by his own dad that no matter your job—even if it was just mopping the floor—you should ignore pain, keep your head down, and do your absolute best. But he'd hated his father, at one point actually plotting to kill him! "I know the feeling," I said without thinking. "I hated you when I was growing up." My father doubled over with laughter. He was a complicated man.

We did not own an automobile until 1955, a used Ford station wagon that no one but my father was allowed to drive. That is, until my mother decided to get her license and buy her own car with money loaned from an aunt. I was shocked to see Mother pull up in her 1947 Chevrolet, my little brother Gregory in the front seat. Dad was even more surprised.

But being an independent-minded woman with three children took its toll. On weekends, mother sometimes disappeared from home to stay at a hotel, telling me where she was but swearing me to secrecy. By Sunday, she'd return to greet us with a delicious Sunday dinner when my dad, brothers, and I returned from church. Years later, she told me that she'd been desperate for some time to herself.

The year after dad bought his car, he purchased our first television set, one of those boxy consoles flanked on either side by built-in bookcases. We were allowed to watch for only a few hours each week. On Saturday mornings, it was chores starting at ten a.m., then a trip to the market for groceries, then dinner—a life so structured and regulated I sometimes felt I was being slowly crushed. On Sundays, Dad woke us for services at Zion Baptist Church by seven o'clock. First came Sunday school, followed by services. On Sunday evening, we returned for more services.

Zion, the first Black Baptist church in Cincinnati, sat in a majestic building on Ninth Street in the West End and hosted many famed preachers—Dr. Martin Luther King Jr., Dr. Howard Thurman, and the Reverend Ralph David Abernathy among them. Our reverend, L. Venchael Booth, was an intellectual whose sermons were considerably shorter than those of the average Baptist minister. Dad found this lack of "hoopin' and hollin'" to be highly commendable.

It was on a Sunday afternoon, coming home from church, that I had my first encounter with overt racism. My parents, as I've mentioned, did not own a car until I was eight, so we took the bus to and from church. On this particular Sunday, we were walking up Ninth Street toward the bus stop. Just as we rounded the corner, we saw the bus a few feet away. But instead of stopping, the driver smirked at us and drove by. In those days, all buses heading toward downtown turned around at Fountain Square and headed back out to the suburbs, so we walked another block and caught the same bus as it was traveling back toward Avondale. "Why didn't you stop?" my father yelled at the driver as we stepped on. "I know you saw us! Was it because we're Black?" I had never seen such a look on his face. The man behind the wheel glared, but remained silent as my dad stormed to the back of the bus where we were already seated, a little scared, a little thrilled, entirely confused.

After we got home, my dad sat me down with Larry and explained that, as Black people, we would be treated inequitably by some. It would not always be easy to tell who was a racist and who was not, he continued. But about one thing we should be absolutely clear: we must never, ever lower our expectation of fair treatment. We were as American as anyone else in this country, with as much right to its opportunities if we were willing to work for them. The conversation left an indelible impression on my seven-year-old mind.

As a child, I'd been aware that my life would be shaped by race. But initially, the clues were subtle. When I asked my father why we never went to the amusement park on the outskirts of Cincinnati he explained that, as Black people, we were permitted inside the park, but not allowed to swim in the pool. If we could not have access to all of the park's amenities, dad said, he was not going to give them his money.

★

Though music was a constant presence in my childhood home, not until junior high school did it become central to my life. I'd grown quite overweight, and I was increasingly self-conscious about it. Despite my early academic accomplishments, I had not followed my classmates to the special college preparatory school they attended. Instead, I was sent to Samuel Ach Junior High, reputed to be one of the toughest schools in Cincinnati. This bewildered me, and I was terribly upset. Over the summer, I wrote a long letter to the principal, Dr. Lawrence D. Hawkins, explaining why I thought Samuel Ach was wrong for me and announcing that I had no intention of attending.

Of course, there I was on the first day of school, and Dr. Hawkins summoned me to his office. He was the first Black man to become a principal in the Cincinnati public schools, and all my bravado melted as I walked the long hallway to his office. A secretary ushered me inside, and Dr. Hawkins reached out with his large hand. I would receive a good education at Ach, Dr. Hawkins promised, and he hoped to see a lot of me. I was dumbstruck. He'd noticed me, taken a specific interest. It was a huge boost to my self-esteem. By stepping forward to connect with a person prepared to be his enemy, Dr. Hawkins became my first real mentor. More than fifty years later, when he and his wife were both in their eighties, they attended my inauguration as the president of Wheaton College.

Later, I learned that I had been eligible to attend the tonier college prep program at Walnut Hills High School after all. But the letter informing me of this never arrived. Instead, it was mistakenly delivered to our next-door neighbors (their address was 3447 and ours was 3447 ½), and because we were not always on good terms with them (my father making no secret of his belief that they brought rodents into the neighborhood), this important piece of mail somehow failed to find its way into our box.

I had no idea of this back story when my school counselor asked why I'd chosen not to go to Walnut Hills. I told him I'd never made that choice; I hadn't even known I was eligible. My counselor did the right thing. He told me I could transfer then and there. But my mother refused to sign the paperwork. "If you weren't good enough for them in the seventh grade, you aren't good enough for them now. Just stay where you are," she said, not yet aware of the postal error and feeling slighted. I was furious. But staying at Ach turned out to be a decision that shaped the rest of my life.

Though I did not know it, the choir at Samuel Ach Junior High was among the best in the state. Clyde Williams, first Black graduate of the Cincinnati Conservatory of Music, was our conductor. He took us to live opera, introduced us to music from around the world, and taught us how to sing in foreign languages. One day, the band director popped in during a rehearsal to announce a new instrumental music program offered that summer at Withrow High School. He said anyone who was accepted would be able to play a musical instrument by the end of those eight weeks. Did anyone in our choir want to learn how to play an instrument? Mr. Babcock asked. My hand shot up. To this day, I don't know why. I had no experience with instruments, and had never imagined playing in a band or orchestra.

Mr. Babcock asked me to meet him after school for a test of my aural abilities. The program would offer instruction in string, brass, woodwind, and percussion instruments. But to determine which we were best suited to, he would need to test our listening skills; only those with the most refined ear could play a string instrument, he said. After my test, Mr. Babcock told me I could choose any instrument I wanted. I had always liked the sound of stringed instruments when my mother took me to hear children's concerts at the Cincinnati Symphony. But I was quite overweight at the time and thought that if I played the violin, I would have to stand up and expose my size. A cello, by contrast, allowed its player to sit, hidden behind the enormous instrument. So that was the one I chose.

Almost immediately, I fell in love with that instrument. I practiced constantly. The plywood cello on loan from school came to feel like my friend. All summer long, I took string classes. Even on a camping trip, when I was prohibited from lugging my cello into the woods, I sat around the campfire "practicing" by placing my fingers on my right forearm and mimicking the movements used for playing. After all the years of regimentation at home, the discipline of practice came easily to me. My cello began to feel like a second self. Mr. Babcock was impressed by my progress over the summer; he thought I played with a particularly beautiful tone. And when school resumed that fall, he arranged to have me perform for school assemblies. All that fall, I carried my unwieldy wooden friend up and down Prospect Hill, between home and school. Other kids made fun of me. They thought I was out of my mind. But my algebra teacher, a pianist in his spare time, gave me an album of solo pieces and asked me to accompany him during school assemblies. Did Mr. Babcock know how much performing improved the self-esteem of a little fat boy? I'll never know. But by June, I had reduced my waistline from a size 40 to a 32!

Toting a huge, heavy instrument up and down the hills of Cincinnati did more than transform my body; it gave me an entirely new sense of identity. By Easter of the ninth grade, having lost more than fifty pounds, I walked into church wearing a new suit and fairly glowed with pride. Around the same time, Mr. Babcock mentioned a state music competition, and with my confidence surging I decided to enter. But I did not tell a soul. I bought the sheet music for Suite no. 1 in G Major by J. S. Bach. At the downtown branch of the Cincinnati Public Library I also found a film clip of Pablo Casals performing it, and studied his every move. Using the footage as a guide, I taught myself to play the first two movements, embellishing them with a bit of vibrato.

Less than a year after taking up the cello, I walked into the orchestra practice room at Miami University, stepped onto the podium, and performed two movements of the Bach suite for the two adjudicators sitting primly in front of me. A woman who would change the course of my life was among them, listening. When Professor Elizabeth Potteiger learned that I had been playing for only eight months, she offered me a spot in the university's summer music camp right then and there. That invitation would end up shaping all my days to come.

In retrospect, it seems a most unlikely path, from raising my hand in choir practice to landing on stage in front of a professor who would shape the rest of my life. Yet, that's how life stories often unfold. Rarely can we see the path while walking it.

Chapter Four:
MUSICAL BEGINNINGS
IN THE CHURCH

"YOU WILL SING 'Holy Bible Book Divine' at evening service," said Mrs. Ruth Mathis, my teacher in the Baptist Young People's Training Union. I was six years old, and had not even joined Zion Baptist Church yet. My parents were members, attracted by the youthful dynamism of Rev. L. Venchael Booth, who'd recently arrived to lead the church. My brother and I attended Sunday school in the morning, and Baptist Young People's Union in the evening. I have no idea how Mrs. Mathis knew that I could sing, or why she asked me to on that particular evening. But back then, everyone in the Black church could sing, or at least that was my impression as a child, so I never questioned Ms. Mathis's command. When the time came to open my mouth, out poured my young boy's tenor. I was not at all nervous; singing came naturally. And

I liked the attention that followed. It was the first time I'd felt the gratification that comes with performing for an appreciative audience.

This hymn would become an enormous source of comfort throughout my childhood. I often had nightmares after attending the wakes of family members or friends who'd died, and whenever I woke—my heart pounding, my mind confused—the words of that song soothed me. All I had to do was to sing the first few lines, and my anxiety would dissolve:

Holy Bible, Book divine,
Precious treasure, thou art mine;
Mine to tell me whence I came;
Mine to teach me what I am.

I continued to sing in church, and eventually joined a small choral group of young people called the Zionettes. We sang hymns, anthems, and gospel pieces at Zion, also performing at other churches around Cincinnati. I was an introverted kid and quite overweight, so the Zionettes became my primary social outlet. In front of them, I was often called upon to sing solos, and I found that I rather enjoyed the attention. My sense of life as a performer was beginning to take root.

During this period, the 1950s and '60s, Zion Baptist Church was at the forefront of the Civil Rights Movement in Cincinnati. In 1952, the charismatic Rev. L. Venchael Booth arrived and invited a series of progressive guest preachers, including Dr. Martin Luther King Jr., Rev. Ralph David Abernathy, Rev. Wyatt Tee Walker, Rev. Gardner C. Taylor, Dr. Samuel Proctor, Dr. Benjamin Mays, and many others. But Zion's embrace of the Civil Rights Movement directly conflicted with the position of the National Baptist Convention USA, which preferred a policy of official detachment.

The tension did not ease. At bottom, it spoke to the future direction of the church itself. Would Zion be at the forefront of this growing social and political movement, or would it concern itself solely with ecclesiastical matters, as the National Baptist Convention expected? These debates over policy were rooted in the founding of the National Baptist Convention itself, which had seceded from the Consolidated American Baptist Missionary Convention in response to Reconstruction-era tensions between whites and Blacks. Of course, conflict pushed aside rarely evaporates, and the National Baptist Convention faced renewed questions about its identity when Dr. King nominated Rev. Gardner C. Taylor for president in 1961, and saw his candidate defeated. Our own Rev. Booth in Cincinnati had supported Rev. Taylor too, and he rallied other churches to attend a two-day meeting held at Zion to discuss the official direction of the National Baptist Convention. Thirty-three delegates from fourteen states arrived at our church, and from this event the Progressive National Baptist Convention emerged.

As an active member of the congregation, my father served in various capacities to support our national visitors, and I followed along to assist. We set up chairs in the social hall and served meals to the guests, proud to be hosting them in our resplendent new building. At the other end was the sanctuary, large enough to hold more than a thousand people. Here, I sat in the back and listened as delegates hashed through the future of our church. Would we tie its ideals to civil and human rights, or keep our identity rooted in religion alone? At bottom, this deliberation centered on whether a church could make a tangible difference in Black people's everyday lives. Even as a child, I was mesmerized by these questions.

Dr. Martin Luther King Jr. preached at Zion several times over the years, and he made a lasting impression. It felt like he was speaking directly to me, though I had only the barest inkling of all he had seen. "The ultimate measure of a man is not where he stands in moments of comfort and convenience, but where he stands at times of challenge and controversy," Dr. King preached on one Sunday morning. He said, "Life's most persistent and urgent question is 'What are you doing for others?'" and I thought about the way my father was always helping the Jewish widows in our neighborhood. His Black friends criticized him for this. In their eyes, our Jewish neighbors didn't give a damn about us, so why should we do anything to help them? But my father waved off their questions. He had his beliefs and would not be swayed.

Another guest minister who fascinated me was Dr. Howard Thurman. He pastored the Church for the Fellowship of All Peoples in San Francisco, one of the first interracial churches in the United States, and at Zion he spoke very slowly, enunciating each word as he exhorted congregations to develop the strength necessary for living in a racist society. He urged listeners to "find the sound of the genuine within you," and this captivated me. To this day, Dr. Thurman remains an influence on my life. His book, *Meditations of the Heart* is one I often give to others.

By now my experiences at Zion were leading me to think less about building a life in music and more toward becoming a minister. All the men I saw as role models were preachers. In addition to handsome Rev. Booth, inspiring Dr. King, and soulful Dr. Thurman, there was Rev. Peter Marshall, Chaplain of the United States Senate, who was a white man. But that didn't bother me. It won't surprise anyone reading these words to learn that I was something of a bookworm as a child, and when I was about ten I found *A Man Called Peter* at the Avondale branch library. It told of Rev. Marshall's life: he'd been a poor Scottish boy who decided to devote his life to Christ after a near-death experience. This intrigued me. Marshall had saved his money to attend divinity school in America. Then, after landing a position at the toney New York Avenue Presbyterian Church in Washington, DC, he bucked the wishes of the exclusionary elders there and opened the church to all people. The congregation flourished. No wonder. Marshall was an extraordinary preacher. He spoke in pithy phrases, and seemed able to reach anyone, from the lowliest janitor to the most patrician US senator. People felt he was speaking directly to their hearts. Two of Marshall's quotes in particular stuck in my mind:

Give to us clear vision that we may know where to stand and what to stand for—because unless we stand for something, we shall fall for anything

A different world cannot be built by indifferent people.

Peter Marshall's story affected me profoundly. I was fascinated by his ability to reach people from every walk of life. I was ten years old, and I had decided: I would grow up to be a combination of Rev. Booth, Dr. King, Dr. Thurman, and Rev. Marshall. I'd been inspired by the snippets of adult conversation overheard during deliberations around the Progressive Baptist Convention, and now here were these men, living it in front of me. They were making a difference in people's lives through service. I wanted to do the same.

Dr. King preached at Zion on a regular basis. He usually came alone, but on one occasion his wife, the vocalist Coretta Scott King, accompanied him. As I recall, Dr. King preached for morning service, and Mrs. King presented a recital in the afternoon. More than sixty years later, I can still remember her voice. The emotion in it raised goosebumps up and down my arms. Afterward, Mrs. Booth, our preacher's wife, sought me out to speak with Mrs. King. She took me by the arm and led me to the front of the church, where a crowd of people had gathered. I remember the way they parted to allow Mrs. Booth through. I remember how she introduced me to Mrs. King, and how I nervously told her that I had just begun to play the cello. Mrs. King looked down at me. She had piercing eyes but a warm smile. "Keep it up. Practice every day," she said. A Black violinist had just been appointed to the New York Philharmonic, Mrs. King added. Maybe I could be next. (She was referring to Sanford Allen, who in 1961 became the first Black musician in that orchestra). There was nothing obviously life-changing about our brief conversation, but after my exchange with Coretta Scott King I began to seriously contemplate the possibility of becoming a professional musician. The impact of models and mentors in our early years cannot be overstated.

More than thirty years later, I met Mrs. King again. I had become a member of the civic engagement group Leadership Cleveland, performed concerts around the world, and possessed vastly more confidence as a musician. Yet I was still daunted by the prospect of speaking to this Civil Rights icon. Our group of sixty-four leaders from Cleveland was mostly white, and the director wanted us to see a Black city in action, so we flew to Atlanta to tour the Carter Center, then the King Center. Our director asked me to present a gift to Mrs. King as a gesture of appreciation. Was I being used as a token? I wondered about his. But I was even more concerned about blurting out the story of our first meeting so many decades earlier, fearing Mrs. King might be upset by this indication of her age. All of my worries were misplaced. I did indeed bring up the recital at our church. I told Mrs. King that it had shaped my formative years as a cellist and instilled a sense of mission that reverberated to that very day. I could not help noticing that my words brought tears to her eyes.

There is no doubt that growing up in Zion Baptist Church afforded me multiple opportunities for development. In addition to singing, I participated in our annual Prince of Peace competition, which involved delivering approved speeches to a panel of judges. The highlight was delivering these addresses before an audience, and I often chose verses with a deeply spiritual message. One of my favorites was a poetically stylized sermon by James Weldon Johnson that began with, *A Prayer from God's Trombones.* I had learned it during fourth grade at South Avondale Elementary School, and never forgot Johnson's rich imagery of a "lonesome valley" and penitents receiving his words "like empty pitchers to a full fountain." Though a born introvert, I was becoming something of a performer.

I have alluded previously to a growing rift with my father over his rigidity. The first place it began to show up was at Zion. Though I resented my parents' formality, I never considered discussing this with them. I never asked why, or what was behind all of their rules. Instead, I acted out. During a youth program at church, I departed from the script and riffed an extemporaneous critique of the way church elders treated young people. "Some people believe that children and young people should be seen and not heard," I began. "I believe that the young people of our church have valuable perspectives to share with our elders, and I implore you to listen to us." There was no particular issue I was pointing at, just the sense that I felt elders should be more open to listening to the perspectives of those they might not agree with. This attracted the attention of many in our congregation. But my father said nothing. Several years later when he was the scoutmaster of Troop 318, I begged to join another troop—any other troop. He refused to sign the paperwork. So, in a rage, I quit—just as I was on the verge of becoming an Eagle Scout, something I'd worked for years to achieve. I thought I was getting back at my father, but I was the one who lost out in the end. I regretted it for years.

Zion was much more than a center for religious observance. It was a community that sought to lift up the lives of its members well beyond Sunday. The Eddie Gilbert Federal Credit Union is a prime example. Named for a fellow layman who had worked with my father to establish a means for encouraging financial solvency among the congregation, it was one of the first church-sponsored credit unions in the nation. After Eddie Gilbert's death, my dad remained as one of the founding officers. Every Sunday after church in a room right next to the deacon's, he made deposits from congregants who had accounts. My brothers and I had savings accounts, too, and in this way I learned about compound interest, building wealth, and the value of thrift.

For all the support that Zion Baptist offered its people, no one in our congregation could have envisioned the chubby boy who stood to sing "Holy Bible Book Divine" growing up to become a leader in higher education. I've devoted a lot of thought to how and why all the strands of my life tied together as they did, and I believe the foundation was laid by my parents, Andrew and Burdella Crutcher, who brought me up in a highly structured, family-centered, deeply devout household. I certainly don't recommend this recipe for everyone. It caused rifts in my family that took decades to heal. But it did teach me the value of hard work, perspicacity, frugality, and integrity. As a child, I did not always appreciate my parents' wisdom and counsel—especially when delivered by my father. But I am grateful today for those lessons. They showed me how to lead a disciplined life, which has, perhaps counterintuitively, allowed for great freedom.

Chapter Five:
BEING READY

EIGHT MONTHS AFTER beginning the cello, I traveled thirty-five miles to Miami University in Oxford, Ohio, where I would perform two movements from the Bach Cello Suite no. 1 in G Major at a competition hosted by the Ohio Music Education Association. I was fourteen years old, staring at a sea of white faces (with the exception of my father who had driven me there), and more nervous than I had ever been. I closed my eyes and pictured Pablo Casals performing the suite in front of a medieval church in France. This seemed to help. Calmly, I intoned the wavering opening notes. Had I realized that one of the people in the audience that day would change my life, it's likely I would have been far less relaxed.

After I had finished performing both movements, I stood up, bowed, and walked over to my case, preparing to put my instrument away. My father and I were just about to leave when an older woman walked up to congratulate me on my performance.

"How long have you been playing?" she asked, without introducing herself. "Who do you study with?" She wasn't a particularly attractive woman. Some people might describe her as plain. But she had a warm smile and twinkly eyes.

"Eight months," I said. "I take lessons at school."

"Just eight months!" she exclaimed. "How would you like to take lessons here at the university, at our summer music camp? My name is Elizabeth Potteiger. I'm a teacher here, and I think it would benefit you immensely."

It strikes me now that this moment, which felt out-of-the-blue at the time, really wasn't. The Bach suite was a piece I'd selected and taught myself to play specifically for the competition. Something about the undulating contour of the melodic line spoke to me, and I'd been practicing it for months. All of that—my feeling for this piece, my determination to communicate what it meant to me—would have come out in my playing. I had prepared, and I was ready.

My father, who had fallen in love with the beauty of Miami's Georgian-style architecture, was thrilled about the prospect of his son spending two weeks on the beautiful campus. And when the music camp concluded, Professor Potteiger told my parents that she would continue teaching me, for free, as long as they could get me to campus each week. I did not know where this might lead, but I knew enough to understand opportunity. Every Saturday morning for the next three years, I boarded a bus and met with the woman who would forever alter the course of my life. I wasn't sure exactly why Liz Potteiger was interested in my playing, but I sensed that she was watching for something in me. From the time I was a fifteen-year-old high school boy until I was a young man of twenty-two, Liz was my teacher, mentor, and guide.

Outside of music, I was moving up from junior high. I had my heart set on Woodward High School, about five miles from my home, because a friend of mine—also a cellist—would be going there. Leon Friedberg and I had attended first grade together at South Avondale Elementary. He was Jewish and spoke Yiddish at home, but those kinds of divides rarely matter to children. In our first-grade class photo, Leon and I are standing side by side and beaming, without the slightest sense that Black kids and white so often separate as they grow. By the time we reached the third grade, Leon had indeed left South Avondale to attend Hebrew school, and we lost track of one another. But as I was walking to a rehearsal with the Junior Civic Orchestra six years later, a man pulled over in his car and asked if I could point him toward the Fairmount Community Center. I was headed there myself, I told him, and he offered me a ride. Today, such a transaction would be seen as impossibly dangerous, but 1962 was a different time. The man said he was taking his son to the same rehearsal, and as I settled into the back seat, the boy introduced himself to me as Leon. Incredibly, neither of us recognized the other, though we shared the same stand throughout that rehearsal. Back home, I described all of this to my mother, asking if she recalled my friend from first grade—wasn't his name Leon? She dug out the old photograph, and sure enough it was the same boy. I brought the picture along to show him at our next rehearsal, and discovered that Leon, too, had wondered if I was the same boy that he'd known back at South Avondale. We laughed at our mutual uncertainty, and then Leon told me about Woodward High. It was a relatively new building, unlike the nearly hundred-year-old Samuel Ach, and it had stellar facilities, he said. His description of it, especially the orchestra program, was immensely appealing. I decided that was where I would go.

Without consulting anyone, not my junior high homeroom teacher or counselor or parents, I wrote "Woodward High School" on the registration forms for tenth grade, including my home address. My street was not in the Woodward district, but I hoped no one would notice. Miraculously, my plan worked! About a month later I received a letter from the principal welcoming me. My parents, perhaps not realizing that Woodward was out of our district, never even questioned me about it. Every day, I hopped on the public bus, since no school bus would come all the way out to where I lived. But it was no trouble. The public bus dropped me right across the street from Woodward's front door.

I loved my new high school. Unlike Samuel Ach, which was very old, Woodward was modern, practically a brand-new building, and though adults rarely realize this, kids notice such things. The quality of a building, its cleanliness and upkeep, makes very clear statements about the value attributed to the students inside it.

At the time, Black students made up less than ten percent of Woodward's population. The school was predominantly Jewish, and it recognized all the Jewish holidays. Our Christmastime concert was called a Holiday Concert, and it featured music I'd never heard before. Each morning before the first bell, the few Black students would gather in a vestibule at the front of the building called "the Ville." But I never felt comfortable among them. I wasn't much for hanging out, a quality that has persisted all my life, but I kept thinking about my father's admonishment to avoid spending time only with Black people. In retrospect, I imagine that many of my Black classmates considered me arrogant. I am certain that some called me "Oreo." But that didn't concern me. I was a bit of a loner anyway.

This ease with my image among peers did not extend to my teachers. I was having great difficulty in Advanced Placement math, and I wanted my counselor, Miss Schwartz, to let me switch into a less challenging class. She refused. I had the intellectual capacity and just needed to work harder, she insisted. At the time, I interpreted her rigidity as evidence that Miss Schwartz disliked me, and I am sure my behavior communicated that attitude. She would be retiring the next year, and I was happy about it. In truth, though, it is clear that Miss Schwartz wanted more for me. Perhaps she was waging her own personal battle against the "soft racism of low expectations." Whatever her motivations, Miss Schwartz had been correct. I worked hard enough to earn an A in that class, and years later I learned that Miss Schwartz had told her replacement to look out for me. I was a "special young man," she'd said. I offer this story to point out that even when we think all evidence points to one conclusion, acting on that belief can be harmful.

The ruse about my address was eventually discovered. Halfway through the tenth grade, I was called to the principal's office, where they informed me that I did not live in the Woodward district. I was mortified. But the principal told me that I could request a special transfer based on my Advanced Placement courses, which were not offered at my assigned high school. I cringe to imagine what might have happened if I'd convinced Miss Schwartz to slot me into the easier math class.

Woodward HS Council on World Affairs, 1965

On weekends, I awoke every Saturday morning in time to catch the 7:40 a.m. bus to Oxford for instruction with Professor Potteiger. When I returned home nearly twelve hours later, I was not at all tired; I buzzed with energy and inspiration from spending all day on a beautiful university campus. Liz Potteiger, meanwhile, was forging a partnership with my parents, and they came to trust her completely. A white woman from the Chicago area, Liz was a vocal advocate for social justice, and active in her local NAACP. She read widely, collected antiques, and traveled to exotic locales around the world. Single and without children, she was entirely devoted to her students and to music. Everything about Professor Potteiger broadened me. She was a founding member of Miami's Oxford String Quartet-in-Residence, and she taught me how to play the cello with my mind as well as my bow. I learned technique, but also the historical background and musical architecture of compositions. Liz called this being a "thinking performer." She taught me how to ensure that what I heard in my mind would actually come out of my cello. That guidance was essential, as I had been primarily self-taught up to that point. Most important of all, Liz taught me about practice. It had to be intentional, specific, and goal-directed, she said. The routine necessary to perform consistently as a musician was analogous to that of an athlete preparing for competion.

Until I studied with Liz Potteiger, the notion of becoming a university professor had never entered my mind.

Since the age of ten, I'd planned to become a minister. Later, I would add architect and lawyer to my list of possible careers. But as I observed Liz, entranced by her life of travel and study, warmed by her presence in my life, I became increasingly convinced that I should consider a similar profession. By the time I entered Miami University as a freshman, I knew two things: I wanted to be part of a quartet-in-residence, like Liz, and I wanted to teach at a university, like Liz. We often pay lip service to the enormous impact of teachers on the lives of young people, though our national policies rarely reflect this belief. I was living it.

After a month of Saturday cello lessons, Professor Potteiger asked my parents for permission to introduce me to a famous musical family then living near Richmond, Indiana. George Klemperer had immigrated from Germany during World War II to study at the University of Chicago. There he met his future wife, Ellen Bartel, a Wellesley alumna, who was working on her master's degree. George and Ellen lived on Chanticleer Farm, a 250-acre parcel of land, where he convened string-quartet "readings" once a week with three other musicians. Liz Poetteiger was one of them, and she wanted George Klemperer to hear me play.

The Klemperer home was warm and cozy, filled with beautiful traditional furnishings. The grand piano sat in a large living room with a roaring fireplace. Mr. Klemperer called all four of his children downstairs to hear me perform, as Liz accompanied me on piano. I had decided to play the Eccles Sonata in G Minor for Cello and Piano, and just before I began the anacrusis of the first movement I happened to glance over at Mrs. Klemperer. She was staring at me in a most unusual way. It was startling, though not frightening. Her gaze simply seemed to look right inside me. Some years later Ellen would become one of my most important spiritual mentors.

Shortly after beginning my weekly trips to Oxford, Professor Potteiger told me that I needed a better cello. The only instrument I'd ever used was a plywood thing owned by my school. But instruments made of plywood are machined, rather than handmade, so they don't resonate as freely as those carved from maple or spruce, Professor Potteiger explained. I didn't know what to do. I wanted the right kind of instrument, but I was fifteen. I had nothing close to the $500 a new hand-carved cello would cost. Back in Cincinnati, I popped into the stringed-instrument repair shop and asked the owner, John Eichstadt, if he had any inexpensive cellos. A former violinist in the Cincinnati Symphony Orchestra, Mr. Eichstadt treated me like the novice I was. He pointed out an older German instrument that cost $250. I felt a cold fear zing through me. *This is an inexpensive instrument?* I thought. In 1962, $250 was a great deal of money, especially to a teenager. How was I going to break this news to my father?

I decided to broach it at the dinner table, where my mother and brother would be witnesses. We had almost finished eating dinner when I nervously looked at my dad and spoke so quickly that he asked me to repeat my words: "Miss Potteiger says that I need to have my own cello." After explaining about the differences in sound between plywood and hand-carved maple, I told my dad about the instrument I'd seen at Mr. Eichstadt's. He agreed to go downtown to the store with me that weekend to buy it. I was so proud. This was the first cello of my very own. It had a soft, brown case, and I took it with me to the Miami University Summer Music Workshop during my second year of participation.

But maybe ten months later, as I was preparing for another competition, Professor Potteiger told me that I had outgrown my first cello and needed yet another new one. I panicked. How in the world could I tell my dad? He would surely refuse. Worse, he would be furious. Again, I went to Mr. Eichstadt, who happened to have three brand new hand-carved German cellos in his shop. Each cost eight hundred dollars. I played all three and chose one that felt and sounded best. It had been made by violinmaker Roman Teller, in Erlangen, Germany, near Nuremberg. I loved this instrument, but I was too afraid of my father to talk to him about it. So I wrote him a note. "Miss Potteiger told me that I need a better instrument. The cello I have is holding me back," I wrote. I also mentioned that Mr. Eichstadt had three new cellos for sale. Maybe we could meet at the store after my competition, I suggested.

I had no idea if my father even read my letter. But I arrived at Mr. Eichstadt's at the appointed time. Had my father been there? I asked. Mr. Eichstadt said no, he had not seen my dad, but he invited me into the back to play the cellos again. As I pushed the curtain aside to peer into the shop's back showroom, there was my father, sitting beside the three cellos. He told me to choose the one that I wanted. I didn't know whether to cry or leap for joy. I could hardly believe what I was hearing. I chose the Roman Teller cello and was so excited that I stayed up all night playing it. Later, I learned that my father had taken out a loan to buy it for me.

Despite these glimpses of his love for me, I'd grown up in fear of my dad, cursing him silently on a regular basis. The thought of actually trying to talk to him never crossed my mind. It was only later that I began to understand what life had been like for him when I was growing up. He was an uneducated machinist, watching his eldest son forge a very different path. As the first Black manager at the Milacron, he'd had problems with white peers, of course. But Black workers treated him even worse, particularly the younger ones. "Just leave me alone, old man," one said, waving him away. My tough old dad was floored by this disrespect. He'd scurried into the men's room, locked himself into one of the stalls, and wept. Had he been riding the young worker too hard? I could imagine that, based on my own experiences with A. J. Crutcher Jr. But his hurt—what was that about? It spoke to something hidden deep within him that would take me many years to understand.

Professor Potteiger had been accurate. I could hardly believe how much easier it was to play on a better instrument, and I made rapid progress. Always trying to get me in front of musicians who could help me along the path, Professor Potteiger arranged for me to play for Dr. Paul Katz, music director of the Dayton Philharmonic Orchestra. She drove me to his home on a Saturday afternoon, and I performed several pieces, accompanied by Professor Potteiger on the piano. Dr. Katz was a short, stout, serious-looking man with a mustache. He reminded me a bit of Albert Einstein. After I'd finished playing, he offered me a position in the Dayton orchestra, a semi-professional group that he had founded. But to become a member, I would need to join the musician's union, specifically the American Federation of Musicians Local No. 1 in Cincinnati.

Joining the guild was quite a process. My father accompanied me downtown to the Local 1 headquarters on Linn Street. In the office sat several older men in black suits. They were not very welcoming and did not appear to be pleased by my request to join. They asked a lot of questions, lectured me about the history of the Cincinnati union (the first musician's union in the United States), and scrutinized my signed contract from the Dayton Philharmonic.

The orchestra rehearsed in the evenings and on weekends at the Dayton Art Institute. I rode to rehearsals with musicians from the Cincinnati Symphony who were also performing in the Dayton group. All were adults. To be a teenager among them felt a bit strange at first. But through our hour-long car rides, I eventually realized that we shared many interests, even beyond music. For my first concert, a program including the Berlioz overture to *Benvenuto Cellini*, the Brahms Symphony no. 4 in E Minor, and the Tchaikovsky Piano Concerto in B Minor with piano soloist Van Cliburn, one of my uncles loaned me his set of tails, and my father taught me how to tie a bow tie. He was about an inch shorter than I, and he stood in front of me, guiding my fingers for the first two attempts. Tying a bow tie was much like tying a shoestring, he said. Then he stood back, smiling broadly as I successfully tied the knot on my own. How proud I was, walking on stage in my elegant black tails and white satin bow tie.

We began each concert with "The Star-Spangled Banner," but I was anxious to get on to the Berlioz. As Dr. Katz raised his baton to begin it, I could hardly corral my excitement. Afterward, though I'd just performed my first concert as a professional, I asked Van Cliburn for his autograph.

Performing in a professional symphony orchestra while still in high school was not without challenges. Proud as they were, my parents worried about the late nights and hours of rehearsal time. What about homework from school? they kept asking. I'd manage by squeezing in work sheets and essays during rehearsal breaks and study halls, I assured them. It worked for a while, but when the symphony began offering school-day concerts for children, the effects on my work showed up immediately. My Advanced Placement math teacher sat me down one day for a very serious discussion. "You are a very intelligent niggra," Miss Anna Spain Davis said in her southern drawl. "We have high expectations of you, and you are going to ruin your chances if your grades do not improve." Again, I felt a strange mix of emotion—both rattled by her words and supported by her obvious care for me. Another time, when I had to dash from the dress rehearsal for a school play to Dayton for a concert, I changed into my tails in the high school dressing room and barely made it to the concert on time. People were gaping at me as I ran into the concert hall, but I ignored this. Not until I finally sat down in the dressing room and looked in the mirror did I realize I was still wearing makeup from the high school play rehearsal.

I continued to make progress on the cello, and by fall of my senior year Professor Potteiger suggested that I audition for the Cincinnati Symphony Young Artists Competition. The winners would perform with the symphony in five children's concerts the following spring. I prepared meticulously for this competition. I memorized the two movements of the Vivaldi concerto in less than a week, and spent hours practicing until every note was imprinted in my brain. Despite all of the work, I was quite surprised to learn I'd earned a spot, along with a high school pianist, a harpist, and a flutist. The many hours of hard work and preparation had paid off. But a few hours after the announcement, Professor Potteiger sat me down for some hard words. People were hailing me, congratulating my performance and professing amazement that I could play so well after just a few years on the cello, yet Professor

Potteiger reminded me that somewhere in the world there were children even younger than I who could play just as well—if not better. I suspect that all the adulation and my sincere pride in having won had gone to my head. *She's right. Come back down to earth,* I remember thinking.

Rehearsing with the Cincinnati Symphony was the musical highlight of my life to that point. Hearing the rich, sonorous tones of the orchestra quite literally transported me. I had become friendly with Sigmund Effron, concertmaster of the CSO, who often invited me to rehearsals when famed string players were performing. But in the spring of 1965, when I walked on stage at the Cincinnati Music Hall and sat down in front of two thousand people to perform the Vivaldi Concerto in E Minor, I faced what might have become a disaster. Vivaldi had written more than one concerto in the key of e minor, and someone had ordered orchestral parts for the wrong piece. No one would have been surprised to see a seventeen-year-old kid flummoxed by such circumstances. But I wasn't nervous. Rather, I felt exhilarated as I sat down and positioned my bow. My accompanist on piano was to be Mr. Effron's wife, Babette, whom I knew well, and Mr.Effron had by then become a mentor to me. I mention these connections to underscore the value of building relationships outside of one's immediate social circle.

The five performances went well. My mother was in the audience for each one, sitting with my younger brother and an assortment of relatives and church members. These young people's concerts were held during the day so my father could attend only one of them. But he brought the concert program to the factory floor at Cincinnati Milacron and passed it around to all the workers. He talked about my concert to anyone who would listen, and a month later, an article about my performances showed up in the Milacron employee newsletter. I had never seen my dad so proud.

The experience of working with a world class orchestra confirmed my goal for the future: I would become a professional musician – no matter how risky or impractical that dreamed seemed to be.

Of all the lessons I've absorbed along my unlikely career path, the importance of discipline is the one non-negotiable, the essential component for anyone who seeks achievement. Psychologist M. Scott Peck has called discipline "the basic set of tools required to solve life's problems," and I subscribe wholeheartedly to this belief. While life is full of happenstance, there really are no accidents and, in the end, no shortcuts. I'd bristled for years against the rules and regimentation of my youth, but the discipline I learned at home, reinforced later by Liz Potteiger, became the foundation upon which I built all that was to follow.

Chapter Six:
On Becoming
An Interdisciplinary Musician

During my sophomore year in high school, I decided again to compete in the Ohio Music Education Association Competition. This was the same competition where Liz Potteiger had first heard me as a ninth grader. It was to be held in Dayton, and neither of my parents could drive me, so a friend, Sue Worrell, invited me to ride with her and her father. Dr. John W. Worrell was music supervisor for Cincinnati Public Schools, and he had played an important role in helping me secure the transfer to attend Woodward High. While I was certainly happy to have a ride to Dayton, I was a little nervous at the prospect of sitting in a car with Dr. Worrell for more than an hour.

On our way to the competition, we made a stop at the home of a friend of Dr. Worrell's. Bill Scutt was a high school string teacher who also played first violin in the

Dayton Philharmonic Orchestra. We were at his home for less than an hour, and nothing there made much of an impression on me—other than the barrage of questions Mr. Scutt asked. He grilled me about my parents: what did my father and mother do for a living? Where did I live in Cincinnati? And with whom did I study? When I told him about Professor Elizabeth Potteiger at Miami University, he appeared utterly flummoxed. As we got back into the car, Dr. Worrell turned to face me in the back seat. I was likely the first Black person ever to set foot in the Scutt home, he said. This rattled me enormously. *What am I supposed to say to that?* I recall thinking. *How should I respond?* Even now, it is difficult to describe my feelings. It was as though I was an alien from another planet—a mysterious being. By the time we got to Dayton, I was utterly drained. How could I possibly perform the Bruch "Kol Nidrei"?

To say I was unsettled when we arrived at the competition would be putting it mildly. To make matters worse, when I looked at the program I noticed that they had my name as "Rona Crutcher." I did not play well. Unlike the previous year, when I'd received a I rating, the highest possible, this time I rated only a II rating, which was middle-of-the-pack. In short order, I began to lose my zeal for the cello. I started singing again, auditioned for the school variety show, and joined the Woodward Ensemble, our school's premier choral group. I became one of the group's tenor soloists and considered putting the cello aside altogether.

Liz Potteiger surely noticed my waning interest, though I continued our lessons. To her credit, she never pressured me to become a music major—just the opposite. When I mentioned an interest in architecture, Liz introduced me to Mik Stousland, head of the Architecture Department at Miami U. Since I was on campus every Saturday from 9 a.m. to 4:50 p.m., when the bus came to take me home, I had lots of free time, and Professor Stousland allowed me to spend it drawing in the architecture studios. I wandered the student union and university library. I thought I was experiencing what it might be like to be a college student.

But Miami University was not my first-choice school. I was aiming for Carnegie-Mellon and the world-famous Oberlin Conservatory of Music. My father had promised to support whatever choice I made, though when he learned that Miami had offered me a full-ride merit scholarship the die was cast. If I chose to go somewhere else, I would have to cover the cost difference myself, my dad said.

I came back to music for good a year after the disaster in Dayton. It was 1965, and I had been chosen as a member of the Ohio Music Education All-State Orchestra, which consisted of the top players from regional orchestras statewide. This was an opportunity to perform with the very best high school string, brass, wind, and percussion players in all of Ohio, and quite an honor. I had been looking forward to it for years. Although the concert conflicted with another that I was to play with the Cincinnati Youth Symphony Orchestra, of which I was now president,

Sigmund Effron, our conductor, graciously excused me. Yet another pivotal decision that looked fairly inconsequential at the time.

The All-State Orchestra performance was held at Capital University in Columbus. We musicians arrived on Thursday afternoon for auditions, with the final concert to be held on Sunday afternoon. My audition went well, I thought, as I walked over to scan the postings a few hours later. I hadn't expected to be named principal cello chair, but I was happily surprised to see that I'd earned the place of assistant principal, meaning that I'd be seated right up front on the stage. Suddenly, I noticed one of the female cellists crying. She'd been named third chair, right behind me. I didn't think much about this. But a few hours later at our first rehearsal, the conductor took me aside. I should move back to sit in the second row, in the third cellist's chair, he said. A demotion, at least visually. The young woman who'd been crying was now elevated to the same level as me—we'd share assistant principal status—but she would be the one most visible. I'd be seated behind her. I was hurt but more than that, perplexed. I just couldn't understand the rationale. *They wouldn't have done this if I was white*, I thought. There was no time to dwell on those feelings, however. What good would it do? And I did get to play one of the solos in the last movement of the Dvorak symphony. Were I able to time-travel back to that moment with the knowledge I have today, I would ask the man who auditioned us why he made the sudden change—if only to see what kind of excuse he'd make.

There were only two other Black musicians in the All-State Orchestra that year, a female bassoonist from Cleveland and a male violinist from Springfield, so I knew the chances of my having a Black roommate were slim. Indeed, I was paired with William Blossom, a white bassist from Cleveland Heights. As we lay in our beds talking after lights-out, he spoke of his determination to become an orchestral musician. He'd already performed as principal bass in the World Youth Orchestra at the famed Interlochen Music Camp in Michigan and, overall, had much broader musical experience than I did. I was in awe.

William Blossom did indeed go on to become a member of the New York Philharmonic, where he enjoyed a forty-year career. It's likely that he never knew how much he'd influenced me that weekend. I'd pined to attend Interlochen, the most famous music camp in the world. I'd even received a partial scholarship from a music club in Cincinnati to further that goal. But it covered only half of Interlochen's eight-hundred-dollar cost, and my father had already bought me a new cello that year. There simply was no more money. But as I listened to Bill talk about the camp, I realized just how much I'd missed by not going. Between that, Bill's enthusiasm for pursuing music as a career, and my own elation at performing with such a high-caliber orchestra, my resolve solidified: I would become a professional musician, whatever it took.

But not until the summer I was to enroll at Miami University did I confess this aspiration to my dad. He'd known about my love of architecture, and I assumed that he wanted me to pursue this more concrete career path. I was afraid he'd consider me wishy-washy, unserious, to turn back toward music. But he wasn't upset at all. "If that is what you want to do, it's fine with me," he said. "Just be sure to take some education courses so you can get a job."

One of the things that had stood out about Bill Blossom was his knowledge of music history and theory. At Interlochen, he'd taken classes in these essential subjects. But other than one week of theory I'd taken during Miami's Summer Music Workshop in high school, I knew nothing about solfege, the study of pitch and sight reading. This hole in my musical education showed up in my ignorance about such basics as the chromatic scale and key signatures.

Miami professor Joseph Bein, recognizing my deficit, agreed to tutor me with a crash course in music theory so that I'd be prepared for the qualifying test before first semester began. Another lucky break. We drilled relentlessly on the fundamentals, and I passed, which allowed me to skip remedial coursework and enroll directly in first-year music theory. It's amazing to me, looking back, at the way such seemingly small moments—an overnight conversation, a professor's generosity—can affect the trajectory of a life.

Truth be told, my first semester at Miami U was not impressive. I felt a bit lost, thrown by the relentless social life, and my grades reflected it. Especially embarrassing was my C- in Survey of Musical Styles, a required course for first-year music majors, in which you had to analyze a piece aurally. We were taught to diagram the contours of the music with a variety of symbols, similar to diagramming a sentence. I just did not get it! But I was too embarrassed to ask anyone for help, a huge mistake since speaking with my professor could have been an opportunity to build a relationship, rather than an admission of failure. I often share this story with mentees as a cautionary tale. Bottom line: when in trouble, do not be proud. Seek assistance. By the start of second semester, I'd learned that one of my high school friends had received an A in the same survey course, so I arranged to study with him—my scholarship might be on the line. Almost immediately, it became clear that in my anxiety I'd made the process far too complicated. If I'd merely arranged a meeting with the professor, I would have learned that he was nudging us to describe the texture of an entire section of musical composition, rather than the microscopic work I was trying to do for each and every measure. I think back on this as a much-needed lesson in humility and also on the importance of comprehending the big picture, rather than fixating on tiny details. I received an A in Survey of Musical Styles that semester, which significantly raised my grade point average.

Around the same time, my academic advisor suggested that I learn German. He told me that if I was going to become a music major I ought to learn the language of the great composers such as Bach, Beethoven, Brahms, and Schumann. I was game, and enrolled in first-year German. As with my old plywood cello, I loved the language immediately. It came easily to me, and at the end of my sophomore year I'd decided to double-major in music and German.

Liz Potteiger was not pleased about this decision. She'd already complained that I was signing up for too many credit hours, which took time away from practicing cello. I was in Miami's honors program, giving me priority during class registration and allowing me into almost any course that interested me—there were so many! Rarely did I have a load with less than twenty hours of coursework per week. But after my bumpy first-semester start, I made it onto the dean's list each semester.

Toward the middle of freshman year, Liz Potteiger told me about an intriguing summer opportunity. George Klemperer, whom I'd met through Liz during our first year of study together, had been killed in an accident at Chanticleer Farm, and his widow wanted to offer me a scholarship in George's memory to attend the Cummington School of the Arts in Massachusetts. Established in 1908, the Cummington School emphasized creative collaboration across the fine arts, offering not just concerts but summer residencies where writers, painters, musicians, and performers of all kinds could practice under the guidance of visiting artists. Among its noted alumni were such luminaries as Helen Frankenthaler, Willem de Kooning, Diane Arbus, Marianne Moore, and Archibald MacLeish. The school also had sparked the founding of Harry Duncan's Cummington Press, which published the early works of Tennessee Williams, Robert Lowell, and Dana Gioia, among others. Having never spent time in the Northeast before, I was thrilled by this prospect. I would also have to provide my own transportation, but other than that, and an extra two hundred dollars, I was covered. Liz Potteiger discussed Ellen Klemperer's offer with my parents, and they agreed that this would be an amazing opportunity.

In June of 1966, I set off on a trip to New York City with Nancy Koutzen, one of Liz's former students, who had been visiting her parents in Ohio and was driving back to the city. I had never been anyplace like New York before, and everyone had advice about what I should expect there. Liz Potteiger encouraged me to spend a few days exploring the city's wonderful arts scene before taking a bus to Massachusetts. George Barron, who was my voice teacher and dean of Miami's School of Fine Arts, told me to spend as little time as possible in New York, and to walk only in lighted areas. I reserved a room for three nights at the YMCA in midtown Manhattan, where I slept every night in my single bed literally hugging my cello. Despite all of this, I had a wonderful time alone in New York. I visited Lincoln Center and the Metropolitan Museum of Art. I walked from Thirty-Second Street up to Harlem, and spent hours just wandering around taking it all in. I had dinner at Sylvia's, the famous soul food restaurant, and walked around Central Park. By the time I left, I had worn out the soles of my shoes; the first thing I did upon arriving in Massachusetts was buy a new pair.

I rode the Peter Pan Bus from New York to Pittsfield, Massachusetts, where Hal and Adelaide Sproul, friends of the Klemperers, picked me up. Hal Sproul had founded Cummington, and he affected a classic New England air, complete with pipe. Adelaide, a comely woman, spoke in a manner to which I was unaccustomed, enunciating each word with an exaggerated but clipped delivery. She reminded me of the actress Katherine Hepburn (one of my favorites), and sounded impossibly sophisticated to my Midwestern ears. The Sprouls had graciously invited me to stay in their home for two nights before the eight-week summer school got underway.

We drove up to a New England-style stone farmhouse located on the edge of the school's property. Adelaide showed me to my room on the second floor and left me to unpack while she went to prepare dinner. My room was furnished traditionally, with heavy drapes framing the windows. I sat down to try out the bed, which was very comfortable, and decided I would feel right at home with the Sprouls. About forty-five minutes later, Adelaide called me down to eat a classic New England meal of clam chowder, baked cod, corn on the cob, and broccoli. We finished with an apple pie and thick slices of cheddar cheese. The Sprouls asked lots of questions about my relationship to George Klemperer's widow Ellen, and even more about my background. But rather than feeling cornered or interrogated as I had in Bill Scutt's living room, I felt welcomed. Differences in intent come through. The Sprouls appeared genuinely interested in getting to know me, rather than viewing me as a dark-skinned curiosity.

The Cummington School of the Arts invited ten visual artists, ten writers, and ten musicians to be in residence for eight weeks each summer. Among the distinguished teaching-artists that summer were former Poet Laureate Richard Wilbur; Sonya Monosoff, a violinist on the faculty at Cornell University; Karen Tuttle, a violist at the Curtis Institute of Music; and George Finckel, a cellist who taught at Bennington College. They were our mentors, all living in a converted barn and houses spread across the rustic property halfway between Pittsfield and Northampton. For two days, I was the only student around. And I spent the time by mopping the floor in the small dining hall, washing all of the kitchen utensils, and generally assisting the staff in the final preparations for opening day.

My accommodations that summer consisted of a large room on the first floor of a converted eighteenth-century barn, adjacent to a cemetery. This location caused me some worry at first, but I soon got over it. Indeed, I had no choice, since I had to walk through the cemetery to classes almost every day. My room furnishings were spare and basic, just a small bed, vanity, and desk. The bathroom, which all the barn residents shared, was located up a set of stairs on the second floor. Across the hall lived a horn player from Amherst College named Ed. One evening as I sat at my desk writing a letter to my parents, I heard a blood-curdling screech from his room. It sounded like someone was trying to kill him. I swung open my door to find Ed standing outside his room, eyes bulging as he pointed at something inside. Someone, most likely Ed, had left the barn door open, and a raccoon had ambled right into his room. I could see the poor creature, its claws dug into the wall near the ceiling, just shaking. I backed away, shut the door, and told Ed to be very quiet when I opened it again. After a few minutes, we heard the raccoon drop with a thud. It's claws scritch-scratched across the floorboards as it scuttered toward the door. I opened it, the raccoon looked up at us, and ran free.

My experience at Cummington was transformative in many ways—musically, intellectually, and socially. George Finckel and I discussed the repertoire that I'd already studied, and he assigned me new pieces to learn, including the complicated Bach Sixth Suite in D Major, the virtuosic Saint-Saens Cello Concerto in A Minor, and the Beethoven Sonata in A Major—all of them part of the canon for cello. Under Karen Tuttle, I learned and performed Beethoven's intricate *Two Eyeglasses Obbligato*, a frolicking, almost jocular composition. After George assigned my pieces (everyone was on a first-name basis at Cummington), he told me to get started and come back when I was ready to play one. In other words, I was on my own—no fingerings or bowings suggested. This was radically different from what I was used to with Liz Potteiger, but I had to adjust. Being forced to explore music on my own and learn it only from the notes on the page, without any other guidance, stretched me both musically and intellectually. I came away from that summer with a deeper understanding of the complexities of music-making, and emerged a more confident and consistent cellist.

But Cummington was very definitely geared toward an interdisciplinary approach. All artists should have a sense of disciplines beyond their own, the thinking went. And I was all for it. I'd enjoyed visiual arts as a child so I was eager for the chance to reconnect with this very different form of communication. At Cummington, I spent a good part of the summer learning to make Japanese woodblock prints. Chris Horton, a graduate student at Wesleyan University, was one of the teaching artists there, and he showed me the entire process of woodblock printmaking—how to use the tools to delicately carve grooves into the wood, how to meticulously spread the ink so that it sat evenly on the surface of the wood. I gave a copy of my first color print to Liz Potteiger, and it remained on the walls of her office at Miami until she retired.

At the end of that fascinating summer, George Finckel and his pianist wife, Marianne, invited me to spend a week at their home in Bennington, Vermont. The Finckels had two sons, both of whom played cello and went on to distinguished music careers. For a week, we did nothing but listen to music, talk about music, and play for one another. By the time I went back to Miami University in the fall, I had no more questions about whether I was on the right career path.

I'd been the only person of color at the Cummington School of the Arts that summer. This experience of being "the only one" was not new to me, of course, and no one at Cummington made overt references to it. But still, there were unexpected challenges to being racially different in a small New England town. For instance, haircuts. After living at Cummington for two weeks, I asked Hal Sproul if he could recommend a place where I might get a trim. In those days, I wore a stocking cap at night and kept my hair, which was wavy, close to my scalp. Hal looked at me awkwardly and shook his head. He'd already inquired about this very question, and discovered that there was no barbershop able, or perhaps willing, to cut Black hair. I was shocked. Among all my worries about spending a summer in the Northeaast, lack of haircuts had never crossed my mind. By the end of August I was walking around with a mane more reminiscent of Frederick Douglas than the close-cropped style of Martin Luther King Jr. that I'd always favored. My mother was speechless when I walked through her front door. Needless to say, I was in the barber's chair within hours of my return.

The experience at Cummington had been so powerful that I seriously considered transferring to Wesleyan. Chris Horton had spoken with me about the famed Connecticut school, and the poet Richard Wilbur, who also taught there, had taken an interest in me at Cummington. He invited me to his readings and brought me along with a group of students accompanying him to the premiere of *Who's Afraid of Virginia Woolf* in Northampton. Some of the movie's opening scenes had been filmed on the Smith College campus, and the theater made sure to note this: ACTUALLY FILMED IN NORTHAMPTON, it advertised in capital letters on the marquee. Wilbur's description of the intellectual environment at Wesleyan—along with what I had learned from Chris Horton—appealed to me immensely. Wilbur even promised to write a letter of reference if I applied as a transfer student. For about two weeks, I was torn. But in the end, my loyalty to Liz Potteiger won out, and I decided to remain at Miami. How might my life and career have been different if I'd taken that path? I sometimes wonder. Wesleyan had one of the country's top ethnomusicology programs, and I'd longed to learn more about African and Black American music as an undergraduate at Miami. Had I transferred, I likely would have become more of a music academic, rather than a performer.

As it was, I was preparing to perform my junior recital at Miami the day that Dr. Martin Luther King Jr. was assassinated, in April 1968. I was standing by my mailbox in Stanton Hall when one of my friends asked me, *Is it true? Have you heard?* I was a resident assistant in the residence hall by then, and I ran to the head resident's suite, thinking back to all the times I had heard Dr. King preach at Zion Baptist. It was just dizzying. When the head resident confirmed that King had been critically injured and was unlikely to survive, I went to my room and wept. I thought of all of the people who looked to Dr. King as their liberator, and wondered if I should cancel my recital that night. But almost as soon as that thought formed, I knew it would be a mistake. Instead, I would dedicate my performance to Dr. King's vision and offer a special piece in his memory, the Bach Adagio from the Toccata in C Major, as an encore. Arranged by Pablo Casals for the cello, the adagio is a beautiful, reverent piece that I deemed appropriate for the moment. Before sitting down to play it, I tried to recreate the sense of peace and calm I'd felt as a child listening to Dr. King's words. I told the audience about the impact that he'd had on my life as a young boy, and how his death had dashed the hopes of Black people for a more just United States.

The next day I received the following letter from my music history advisor, Professor Cummings:

Dear Ron,

Thank you for one of the truly moving experiences in our lives. There have been
and there will be many tributes, but none will surpass yours in genuine dignity
and beauty.

The martyr, ours as well as yours, perhaps brings closer in death the realization
of his vision than in life. We certainly hope so.

Sincerely,

Jack and Elizabeth Cummings

Over the following week, I joined two marches in Dr. King's memory—my first time participating in any kind of public demonstration. I was determined to find a way to keep the embers of his audacious dream burning.

★

Halfway through junior year, my German advisor mentioned a new faculty member who had just been hired. She'd received her PhD in German from Stanford University, but her undergraduate degree came from Fisk, an HBCU in Nashville. I'd been too embarrassed to ask directly if she was Black, but I remember my heart fluttering at the thought of this possibility. Professor Katherine Lee had only just been appointed so she didn't yet have any specific courses listed for fall semester. But I happened to walk by her classroom one day, and watched her teaching Goethe. My crush was immediate. I'd been enrolled in another section of the same course taught by my German advisor, but I immediately switched to Professor Lee's class. She was indeed beautiful, but also very engaging as a teacher. Kathy Lee had been a Woodrow Wilson Fellow at Stanford, and as I began to think about applying to graduate schools, I sought her guidance.

The idea of advanced study in music was even more unfamiliar to anyone in my family than studying cello had been, so I was largely on my own. I'd taken a music honors course to prepare for further studies in musicology, and my academic advisor, who'd attended Harvard, urged me to follow in his footsteps. But when I visited the campus, I learned that there would be little time to actually practice cello. The program was focused on the academic study of music (musicology and music theory), not so much about music itself. This did not sit well with me.

But I'd heard that Yale's music program, where Aldo Parisot was a cello professor, operated quite differently. I'd had mentors who raved about Parisot's teaching. I knew who he was, of course, because I had one of his recordings in my record collection; he was considered one of the great cellists of the twentieth century. But I'd no idea that he also taught. I began researching. I learned that Parisot had come to the United States from Brazil to study at Yale as a young man, and eventually replaced his own teacher at the school. Yale was starting to look better and better. It offered courses in musical performance at the School of Music and in musicology through the Department of Music. These distinctions will sound like semantics to a non-musician, but they are not. The best analogy I can offer is the difference between studying Creative Writing and English Literature.

I contacted Professor Parisot and asked if I could play for him after interviewing for a Ford Foundation fellowship in New York City. He agreed. Parisot showed up at his Yale studio with a cello and suitcase in hand, en route to a concert that evening. I played the first two movements of the Dvorak concerto; some of the Beethoven Sonata, op. 69; Bach Suite no. 3; and part of the Barber Sonata. These compositions showcase a broad range of styles and techniques, and I was determined to demonstrate my overall skills. Professor Parisot accepted me as a student on the spot. A few weeks later, I received my official letter of acceptance from the dean of Admissions.

It was at this moment that Professor Lee offered a piece of advice that I shall never forget: I might feel intimated by graduate school, she said. But I needed to know that others were having similar feelings—even if they never showed it.

I completed my undergraduate studies at Miami as a double major in music and German Language and Literature. Although Liz Potteiger had been exasperated to learn I was taking on an additional course of study in Arts and Sciences, it was important to me intellectually. In large part, this new broadening was a result of my experiences at Cummington, where I'd seen the value of cross-disciplinary studies. Liz's mentorship had been key to my ending up there, and I wanted to leave Miami with wider horizons—intellectually, artistically, and socially. We clashed over this, and a number of other issues. But I believe Liz understood what I needed. Her dearest wish—even beyond my becoming an accomplished cellist—was that I build a fulfilling life.

★

When I arrived at Yale, I thought that I had died and gone to heaven! I was learning from world-renowned musicologists like Claude Palisca and Leon Plantinga, while also taking architectural history from Vincent Scully. The range of things to learn was just thrilling. But as I began increasingly to view myself as a scholar, I could not avoid thinking about my relationship to classical music as a Black man. For all of my years of immersion in music—from the church chorus to high school ensembles, statewide competitions, and my studies with Liz Potteiger—I knew almost nothing about the music of Black Americans, or their contributions to the classical canon. The composer Alvin Singleton was in those days my closest colleague at Yale, and together we founded the Black Music Students Union to demand that the School of Music teach a course in African-American Music.

Alvin was a composition major from Brooklyn, who had come to music rather circuitously. He'd worked several years as an accountant, and then enrolled at NYU in his twenties. His was a life so different from my comparatively formal, sheltered childhood. Alvin often invited me to his apartment to introduce me to jazz, schooling me on what was happening in contemporary composition, often playing the pieces several times over. It was a bit overwhelming. Initially, I had a hard time listening to it, but Alvin's repertoire began to grow on me. One day, he asked if I would consider performing one of his original compositions in a recital. What would I be agreeing to? I wondered. I had no idea what might come out of his mind, or how I might sound playing it. But I was intrigued enough to agree.

The piece, "Argoru II for Solo Cello," was to be the second in Alvin's *Argoru Series*. "Argoru" is a word from the Twi language of Ghana meaning "to play." But playfulness was not much in my reporitoire at the time. Alvin and I spent hours together as I tried out different portions of his composition. It was, like all of Alvin's music, heavily influenced by jazz and very improvisatory, so I had to get used to a different style of working. He asked me to try new techniques, creating a variety of musical effects, and he would make changes in the score based on my responses to what he had written. In several passages he wanted me to play using the wood of my bow as opposed to the hair. Then, when I demonstrated the sound, Alvin decided that my left-hand articulation made the notes so clear that the bow should be tossed altogether. He would have me articulate the sounds only with my left hand. On-the-fly composition—it was strange for me, but undeniably thrilling.

I premiered "Argoru II" during my first recital at Yale, on December 11, 1970. The audience clearly enjoyed the piece, and there was lots of buzz about it afterward. I performed "Argoru II" again about a year later in New York City for a composers' forum. And long afterward, in a 1985 concert at Carnegie Hall honoring Alvin's music, I played the piece one last time. The reviewer from the *New York Times* called it "a virtuosic exaltation of the instrument's capabilities." Beyond the pleasure I always felt at pleasing audiences, working with Alvin had stretched my musical boundaries well beyond anything I'd anticipated back at Miami U.

I was fortunate while at Yale to spend two summer semesters at Indiana University, studying with the world-renowned Hungarian cellist János Starker. I had met Starker while at Miami, when Liz Potteiger brought me and some other students to a cello gathering at his campus. Liz had been one of Starker's first American students, and they seemed to have a good relationship. Aldo Parisot also was close to Starker, and in the summer of 1970, they'd arranged an informal exchange: another student and I would attend Indiana U for the summer, and one of Starker's students would take classes at Yale.

Those two summer semesters were pivotal to my development as a cellist. Starker was not nearly as warm and welcoming as Parisot, but he spoke freely around me and I took copious notes. The gist of his instruction was that technique and virtuosity should be used in service to the music, not the other way around. During one lesson, Starker looked at me after I had finished playing and said in his thick Hungarian accent: "Tell me, Ron, how does she do it?" I must have looked puzzled, because he went on to say: "You know, Liz Potteiger. She is not a great cellist, but she has produced some really fine musicians— what's her secret?" I was dumbfounded, both honored and embarrassed, particularly for Liz. I stumbled a bit in answering, but told him that she treated every student as an individual and tried to help them to grow, in whatever way would realize their full potential. The mark of a true teacher.

Chapter Seven:
THE SIGNIFICANCE OF MENTORING

I HAVE BEEN fortunate to have had some truly amazing mentors throughout my life, including a few white teachers in elementary school, and my experience of educators was mostly good. My third-grade teacher, Flora Nichols, announced in front of the class that I was good enough at math to consider becoming an engineer. Being singled out for praise, especially by a white teacher, pleased me, and I went straight to the library to read about engineering. But engineering didn't sound all that interesting. Paging further in the career handbook, I came across "architect." This was far more appealing, as I was good at drawing, and architecture felt like a natural combination of art and math. Though only eight years old at that point, I'd decided: I would become an architect. I can thank Mrs. Nichols for instilling that early academic confidence. On the other hand, she also told us Uncle Remus stories. One line in particular has stuck in my mind all these decades later: "Uncle Remus, you the best storyteller in the whole Nunited States of Georgia!" one child in the story said. I distinctly recall my embarrassment for the little boy, appalled at his ignorance and horrified that people were laughing about it.

There was also Donald Babcock, the band and orchestra director at Samuel Ach Junior High School, who'd told me that I had near-perfect pitch. Despite these generally positive experiences, none of my white teachers had the sustained impact on my development that Liz Pottciger did.

When I began studying with her, Liz Potteiger lived on the first floor of a Georgian house not far from High Street in Oxford. I would walk two blocks from the Ohio Bus Lines bus stop to her home filled with antiques. It was a cozy, welcoming place. Liz oftened asked about my life outside of cello playing, and though she never said so explicitly, these inquiries implied that she cared about me as a person, an individual with a growing mind. She was interested in my favorite subjects in school, and in my church activities. When I mentioned my interest in architecture, she arranged for me to meet Professor Mik Stousland, chair of the Architecture Department at Miami. Professor Stousland toured me around the architecture studios and let me hole up there, drawing, after my music lessons. Liz found it fascinating that my mother's family had held reunions every year since 1916, and she was rapt at my stories about our two hundred relatives gathering each summer.

It was not until I was twenty, and a junior in college, that the issue of race came between Liz and me. Despite her close relationship with my parents and all she knew about my life, we had never spoken directly about my being Black or how that might affect my life as musician. I was the one to raise the topic, and it was sparked by the simple act of reading. During my junior year at Miami, I'd discovered the *Autobiography of Malcolm X,* written with Alex Haley. The book had a profound impact. That someone with such a chaotic upbringing—losing both parents while still a child, then being raised in foster care and dropping out of middle school—could galvanize profound social change, impressed me enormously. Malcolm's later renunciation of the Nation of Islam following his Hajj to Mecca, and eventual transformation to embrace the Civil Rights Movement struck me as extraordinary. But it was his message that resonated most: Blacks needed to look out for ourselves and not depend on white people, he believed. This notion rattled around inside my mind for quite a while. Eventually, it pushed me to start questioning my own behavior and that of everyone around me.

I thought back to my days at the "Ville," where the Black students had congregated at Woodward High School. I am an introvert, as I've said, and don't naturally gravitate toward groups. But after reading *Malcom X*, I wondered why hadn't I taken time to befriend my Black classmates. The same tendency had made me reluctant to join the Black Students Association at Miami University. My father had always counseled us to make a point of talking with white people and avoid interacting only with other Blacks. But I'd taken this to heart with such determination that I often spoke *only* with the white people in any room—actually excluding Blacks.

Growing up in Cincinnati, I'd been aware of racism, but in a hushed and muted way. As a boy, I learned that my uncle had been killed by white police officers while he and another man were delivering furniture. The officers thought they were stealing, rather than delivering those tables and sofas, I was told, and this story terrified me. Until that moment, I hadn't realized that an innocent person could be hurt by people charged with enforcing the law. (Only many years later, during a conversation with my ninety-year-old aunt, did I learn the truth: my uncle had been beaten to death by police at the Cincinnati jailhouse after being accused of raping a white woman. Another woman was on her way to provide an alibi, testifying that my uncle had been at home on the evening of the assault. But he was dead by the time she got there, leaving my two young cousins without a father.)

The more tolerable version of the story was still frightening enough that I began to look at police with fear and suspicion. Soon afterward, two teenage boys from our church had been shot to death by the police while seeking shelter from the rain in the alcove of a jewelry store. The officers thought they were trying to break in. One of the boys had been a friend of mine, and it occurred to me suddenly that I, too, could be killed by a policeman. Everyone in our church was shaken by the Jennings brothers' deaths. But no one talked about it, at least not to me. The terror accompanying this realization is difficult to describe now, at a distance of some sixty years. But it took root, growing in the silence.

As I think back, I am not entirely sure why I avoided the Black Students Association at Miami, but I suspect it stemmed from my concern about being viewed as "other." I was attending a predominantly white university, and I wanted to fit in. I did not want to be singled out as different in any way. Every day, in every class, a constant refrain played through my head: I would show my white classmates that I was just as smart as they were.

But now, galvanized by Malcolm X's story, I thought back to the ways my family had handled race. Was it best to confront it head-on, as my father had done when he stormed up to the bus driver and accused him of racism because he'd failed to pick us up? Or was it better to follow my mother's more restrained approach?

In temperament, my parents were opposites. My mother spoke very properly, while my brash and bombastic father crucified the King's English. Although my mother never explicitly told us to avoid speaking like him, she constantly corrected me and my brothers for our pronunciation and grammar. In the presence of adults, our behavior needed to be impeccable. And our clothes—even when playing with friends—were always quite formal. Because Larry and I were less than eleven months apart, Mother usually dressed us as though we were twins, often with bow ties. Only many years later did I understand that my mother was trying to protect us from precisely the kind of attitude toward Blacks that we'd seen from the bus driver. She would make sure her children gave no one the slightest excuse for demeaning or ignoring us.

But as a college student all of this prim propriety enraged me. It felt unnatural, forced, and when I spoke with my cousins, I expressed myself in a manner my mother would have found deeply unbecoming for cultured Black folk. Yet, to me it felt liberating.

As I contemplated Malcolm X's book, it dawned on me that I was navigating between two poles regarding my sense of self as a Black man in America, and I did not feel quite authentic with either group. Worse, despite all my efforts, I *was* being singled out. I was precisely the kind of "Prize Negro" that Malcolm described with such bitterness. Often, I was the only Black student invited by the president's office to certain events. This became painfully evident during a luncheon with Patricia Roberts Harris who, as US Ambassador to Luxembourg under Lyndon Johnson, had been America's first Black envoy. Although I was the only other Black person in the room—and had been seated directly across from Harris— she ignored me throughout the meal. It was humiliating and confusing. But as I think back to it now, I do not believe there was any hostility in Harris's actions, at least not toward me. I suspect that she recognized exactly why I'd been seated across from her and simply refused to play along.

All of this was swirling through my head, and I was increasingly confused about how to behave, increasingly angry about the way I'd been raised. I didn't know what to do with these complicated feelings, and I spoke to no one about them. Instead, I laid them all at the feet of the white person closest to me, Liz Potteiger. It came in the form of a scathing letter I wrote to her after graduation. I accused Liz of being negligent as a mentor for failing to talk with me about the realities of racism. I blamed her for allowing me to be so clueless. I told her that as someone who was such a champion of Black people she must have been aware of what I was experiencing, and should have talked to me about it. After that, I ceased all communication with her.

Though I'm ashamed of those accusations now, writing the letter to Liz was cathartic. Finally, I had confronted the truth about American racism, and wanted her to know that her attempts to shield me had failed dismally. I was furious as I wrote. But the moment I put the letter into a mailbox, I felt remorse. I knew I should have had this discussion with her in person. Liz, being the wise person she was, wrote me a short and understanding note, making it clear that the door to our friendship remained open. But it would be up to me to walk back over the threshold.

At Yale, my awakening continued. I participated in protests to free Black Panther Bobby Seale when he was on trial in New Haven. I tasted tear gas for the first time on the New Haven Green. Outside a concert given by the New Haven Symphony Orchestra, I handed out "Free Bobby Seale" flyers, and ran into two of my white former classmates from Miami who now had jobs teaching in the Connecticut suburbs. They were shocked to see me with an Afro, my old bow ties banished.

Despite the fact that I was not communicating with Liz, she continued to send me occasional letters. About a year later, I finally wrote back, apologizing for the manner in which I'd severed our relationship. I knew how far I'd come since my first year in college, and I wanted to share with her the transformation I was experiencing at Yale. In that sense, Liz was still my mentor. She had never really left my mind. We had a long telephone conversation about all of it. Liz told me I had been right to be upset with her for failing to open my eyes to the realities outside our little teacher–student bubble. She'd tried to shield me out of worry that these issues might divert my focus from music. Beyond that, she'd been at a loss—how could she guide me with respect to race? Protecting her student seemed the best she could do.

This conversation changed our relationship forever. It turned us into something closer to colleagues. I told Liz about co-founding the Black Music Students Union at Yale because I'd been dismayed to realize that I knew almost nothing about Black music, despite my Bachelor's degree in music. At Miami, we'd learned a bit about jazz and some about William Grant Still, the first Black person to conduct an American symphony orchestra. But that was it. I'd arrived at Yale determined to learn more about Black contributions to classical music, and Alvin Singleton, my co-founder in the Black Music Students Union, had similar goals. I told Liz that we'd met with the dean to convince him to hire a professor who could teach us. Carman Moore, a Black composer from New York City, was eventually signed up. In his course, each of us was assigned to research and write a book chapter on Blacks in classical music. Mine focused on the nineteenth century. Eileen Southern's classic, *The Music of Black Americans*, had not yet been published, so I had to depend on much older sources like *Negro Musicians and Their Music*, by Maude Cuney-Hare, and *Music and Some Highly Musical People*, by James Monroe Trotter. Liz was fascinated and promptly purchased the Cuney-Hare and Trotter books to learn more.

Shortly before I was to complete the final recital and oral examination for my doctoral degree, Liz and I had another long conversation. Two of my friends had just failed their final exams for a supposed lack of music history knowledge. Another friend had just barely passed. The orals were extremely difficult, he told me, focused on questions about music history and theory so detailed they bordered on minutia. I was pretty agitated about all of this—both worried and angry—because I felt that Yale had failed two talented composers for arbitrary reasons. Thinking about my own upcoming orals left me quaking. Though I felt confident about the quality of my playing, I was intimidated by the prospect of sitting for an examination after the recital. The scope would be broad—the entire fields of music history and theory—and frankly, I doubted myself. Although I was embarrassed to admit this to Liz, deep down I wasn't sure I had the intellectual ability to pull it off. I wondered if I should just abandon my pursuit of a doctoral degree, rather than face public humiliation.

I verbalized very little of this, but Liz seemed to sense my crisis of confidence. A week later, I opened my mail to see that she'd sent me a Howard Thurman meditation, "As Long as a Man Has a Dream in the Heart." With it, she enclosed a note that I keep to this day. "I will always remember our last long telephone conversation," she wrote. "For me, the dream has come true! You have found your way home again after a difficult, perilous journey few can ever make. And those who do take the journey rarely find the happiness that comes at homecoming…. It follows, of course, that the artist now is revealed."

Again, she was showing up as the best kind of mentor. Liz's note gave me renewed energy and resolve to complete my degree. I had done everything possible to prepare, and if the committee didn't see me as deserving, so be it. I knew I would be fine either way.

Occasionally, I still pull Liz's note from the Thurman meditation as a reminder of the critical role that she played in my life, how perceptive she was and how deeply she cared about me. That piece of paper is the only object I have to remind me of her significance.

I try now to pay it forward by mentoring students myself. Sometimes this work is informal, simply working with the children of friends and acquaintances. But in 1999, my wife, Dr. Betty Neal Crutcher and I decided to make a more official program of our mentorship, each of us working with a single-sex cohort of students, with whom we meet once a month. It has kept me connected with young people, even when my duties in fundraising and administration take me away from the classroom. More than that, it is my way of honoring Liz Potteiger and the power of mentors to shape a young person's life.

Liz passed away suddenly just a year before I returned to Miami U as provost and executive vice president in 1999. She'd had respiratory problems all her life, and they finally took her. She'd planned to come see me in Austin, three years earlier, to hear Dan Rather speak. But a week beforehand she called to say she was on oxygen and unable to fly. The next fall, in November of 1997, my trio performed at Miami, and I stayed at Liz's home, where she was still tethered to an oxygen tank. She was struggling to breathe, but we still had wonderful conversations. She was fascinated to learn that I'd developed a bond with Bryce Jordan, who was legendary in music education. When I told her that Bryce believed I was destined to become a college president, she said she'd known the same thing for years. She'd hoped I might eventually become the president of Miami U. I was shocked. She'd never so much as hinted at this before.

Normally, I would have stayed with my Klemperer trio colleagues at their family farm in Indiana. It would have been much more convenient. But Liz wanted to see me, and we hadn't had the chance for a face-to-face conversation in nearly ten years. Did I know it would be our last time together? Maybe. Though she was short of breath, we talked about our relationship over the years. Liz said that from the first moment she'd heard me play in the Ohio Music Educators competition, she'd recognized my musicality. And she confirmed what I had long suspected: she'd invited me to the summer music workshop as a teenager to observe my work habits and gauge my long-term potential.

Liz passed away a few months later, just after her seventy-seventh birthday, a day after my own. I'd been booked on a flight to London that day, so I sent my brother Greg to her memorial in my stead. I often second-guess that decision now. One of the bittersweet aspects of returning to Miami as provost and executive vice president for Academic Affairs was that Liz wasn't there to see this culmination of the effect she'd had on influencing a life.

Chapter Eight:
ALONE BUT NOT LONELY

DURING MY THIRD year as a graduate student at Yale, I was working on two doctorates simultaneously: a Doctor of Musical Arts in Performance, and a Doctor of Philosophy in Musicology. My undergraduate studies at Miami had been similarly bifurcated with a double major in Music and German, and I'd been elected to Delta Phi Alpha, the German Honor Society. But I'd never learned to speak German as fluently as I wanted. So, while at Yale, I decided on a whim to apply for a Fulbright Fellowship to Germany. My chances of getting it were about fifty-fifty, my advisor said. It seemed worth taking that shot.

I told no one in my family about this idea. My parents had been perplexed by my interest in the German language all along, though when I finally told them about my double-major, I learned that there had been others in our family drawn to Germany. My paternal grandfather had a brother who'd married a German woman he met during WWI, but no one had heard from him in years.

In my Fulbright application, I wrote that I wanted to study with Siegfried Palm at the Cologne State Academy of Music because he was the world's foremost performer and commissioner of twentieth-century cello music. At Yale, I had become particularly interested in performing contemporary pieces. They felt relevant to me in a way that antiquated compositions did not. So I sent a recording of myself playing a piece written for me by my friend Alvin Singleton, and because we were required to include something from a Baroque composer, I offered my performance of the Eccles Sonata, the first piece that Liz Potteiger had ever taught me. To my astonishment, I was granted a Fulbright Fellowship and took a leave of absence from Yale's musicology program. The decision to veer from my once-linear path was unusual for me, but I was becoming more comfortable with trying new things and letting my interests take me where they would.

I hardly knew how to contain my excitement at the idea of living abroad for an entire year. But in front of my parents, I kept this eagerness to myself. I did not want them to know just how eager I was to leave the country. In fact, although I'd received notification about the Fulbright in February, I mentioned nothing about it to my mother and father until the semester had ended and I was back home in May. They congratulated me, but I could tell from their questions that they were nervous. How would I get to Germany? Where would I live? How would I stomach German cuisine? It wasn't until many years later that I learned how truly frightened my mother was. She worried that as a Black man I might be harmed, even killed, in Germany, though she hid this from me at the time.

I had traveled in Europe once before, in 1969, as part of Miami University's A Cappella Singers. But that was only for five weeks. This trip would be by far the most time I'd ever spent abroad. I departed for Germany in July 1972, on a Lufthansa flight from New York, eager to immerse myself in German culture, and feeling a kind of excitement I'd never experienced before. But there were bumps in the road almost immediately. The Fulbright Commission hadn't thought to book a separate ticket for my cello, so the instrument that had been my anchor and companion for the previous nine years traveled on another flight. While I flew from JFK to Frankfurt and then on to Cologne, my cello was sent to Frankfurt, then loaded onto a truck and driven a hundred and ten miles to meet me at the Fulbright orientation in Bad Godesberg. To say I was unsettled for the entirety of this twenty-four-hour period would be putting it mildly.

There were, as I recall, sixty-four of us Fulbrighters gathered at the Hotel zum Löwen. Dr. Christoph Sattler, assistant director of the German Fulbright Commission, welcomed us as we gathered for dinner. A handsome man with a mop of black hair, Dr. Sattler appeared to be in his late twenties—not much older than most of us students—and he encouraged us to call him by his first name. As he lifted a toast before our first meal, Christoph urged us to take full advantage of our year away from America, not only through study but by getting to know the people of Germany and traveling the country as much as possible. I remember thinking that I needed no encouragement; I could not wait to explore.

Our meal that night was *Rinderrouladen*, a beef roll filled with bacon, onions, mustard, and pickles, browned and simmered in rich gravy. On the side, a plate of sweet-and-sour red cabbage. Both dishes are traditional German fare, but I had never eaten anything like them. I was enjoying it all immensely, though I'd noticed that the waitress hesitated as she served me. "Ist gut, oder moechten Sie etwas anders?" she asked, pointing to my plate. (Is this okay, or would you like something else to eat?) I was the only Black person at the table, and she hadn't posed this question to anyone else so I imagined snapping, "No, please get me some fried chicken." But I muffled that impulse and told her the meal was fine for me.

After dinner, we adjourned to another room to learn which of several Goethe Institutes we'd been assigned to for language instruction. There were several, scattered all over the country, and I listened for my name as Dr. Sattler sent students off to Göttingen, Freiburg, Munich—all kinds of interesting cities. Finally, he turned to me and sighed, in English. "You have been assigned to Iserlohn." Then he added: "Es tut mir leid." (I am sorry to have to tell you.)

I had never even heard of Iserlohn. I looked it up on a map and saw that it was located in the middle of the Sauerland, a hilly, heavily forested area spreading across much of North Rhine-Westphalia. In this sparsely populated region, Iserlohn was the largest city. When I arrived there with four other Fulbright fellows in July 1972, the lone movie theater was playing a seventeen-year-old film, *Rebel Without a Cause* ("...denn Sie wissen nicht, was Sie tun"), from 1955. In Iserlohn, that passed for contemporary culture.

In each of the assigned cities, we scholars would have two months of language instruction, speaking nothing but German for six hours a day. Within three weeks, I was dreaming in German. I saw myself standing with one of my classmates in her parents' kitchen as they asked me: "wie gefaellt ihr Deutschland?" (How do you like living in Germany?)

Was I honest in the dream? The truth was that I felt I might never find a way to fit in there. My roommate at the Goethe Institute was an African-American electrical engineering graduate from the University of Illinois Urbana–Champaign (we were two of only three Blacks in the entire program), and every day as we walked to the Goethe Institute people on the streets stared. We usually gathered with other Fulbrighters for lunch and dinner. But I spent the bulk of my time studying. There simply wasn't much else to do in that small town. By the end of time there, I felt much less optimistic about spending a full year in Germany. I wondered if I had made a mistake.

In 1972, of course, there was no Internet, and while I'd previously called home to talk with my parents once a week from Miami and Yale, as well as frequent check-ins with Liz Potteiger and Ellen Klemperer, the only public pay phone in Iserlohn was at the post office. Moreover, international calls were prohibitively expensive. In America, I'd spent hours at Chanticleer Farm, sitting with Ellen as we listened to tapes of Howard Thurman reading his meditations. Now alone as never before, I realized how much I'd depended on those conversations for stability and connection. I was learning so much in Germany, thinking so many new thoughts, and I wanted to share them. But the only practical way to do this was through letters and post cards. I wrote many, week after week.

In Germany, college-level schools don't begin their fall semester until October, so I had two months of free time. The Fulbright Commission had arranged for those of us without other plans to live with families for a month as part of the Experiment in International Living. I was assigned to live with the Dahmann-Keusens in Mehlem, a small town just outside of Bonn. Herr Dahmann-Keusen, an architect, and his cellist wife, Ursula, lived just two blocks from the Rhein River. It sounded idyllic.

At the train station I recognized Frau Dahmann-Keusen immediately. She was a tall, striking woman with a rather long face, who'd taught at the Bonn Music School for years. As she motored down the B-9 highway to Mehlem, we chatted pleasantly in German. "How did you like Iserlohn?" she asked right off the bat. I was honest. I would have preferred Munich or Tübingen, I told Frau Dahmann-Keusen. "Furchtbar!" she replied (How awful!). "I cannot believe they assigned you to such a terrible city." Then came the usual questions about my family: Where had my parents been born? How many siblings did I have? Frau Dahmann-Keusen was merely trying to make conversation. But it felt like I was on the hot seat. As we made our way down the highway, she pointed out a series of drab government buildings (Bonn was then the capital of West Germany). The sights became more interesting after we entered Bad Godesberg, where the streets were lined with lovely homes. History was everywhere. Frau Dahmann-Keusen explained that her family had once owned most of the land from the highway down to the shore of the Rhein River. I did not immediately appreciate the significance of this information, but it soon became clear.

We made another turn onto a small gravel road. On the right side were houses, and on the left, fields of crops stretching as far as I could see. We pulled up in front of a contemporary, white stucco home with black window frames. Frau Dahmann-Keusen opened the door, and her husband rose to greet me. Herr Dahmann-Keusen was a pleasant-looking man with thick eyebrows. He was smoking a cigar and wearing an Austrian Loden jacket.

"How is it that a Black man who grew up in the ghetto learned to play the cello?" he said, reaching out to shake my hand.

This was not at all the greeting I had anticipated. It nearly knocked me off of my feet. I'd been there less than five minutes and already uncomfortable. But I maintained my composure and explained that I had not, in fact, grown up in a ghetto. I described our home and neighborhood in Cincinnati, pointing out that we were only the second Black family on the street. This rather inauspicious beginning was only a harbinger of things to come.

At the Dahmann-Keusens' awkward situations cropped up at the most innocuous-seeming moments. One day during the midday meal, the entire family broke into song: "Zehn Kleine Negerlein, die wollten uns regieren!" they sang to the tune of "One little, two little, three little Indians." This was the campaign song for candidate Rainer Barzel, who was running for Chancellor. (Roughly translated, it said, "Ten little Black people want to be our leaders!")

"Ronald, warum singst du nicht mit?" Frau Dahmann-Keusen asked. (Ronald, why are you not singing with us?)

I was extremely uncomfortable. Between my otherness, my still-weak German language skills, and the fact that I was essentially captive in this home, I stumbled to explain, delicately, why, as a Black man, I was offended by the lyrics.

"Oh Ronald," Frau Dahmann-Keusen laughed, "it's only a song!"

That year, 1972, was a pivotal in German politics. Rainer Barzel, my hosts' preferred candidate for chancellor, was challenging incumbent Willy Brandt, a former journalist who'd opposed the Nazis. I knew about Brandt because he'd recently won the Nobel Peace Prize for his work encouraging reconciliation between West Germany and the countries of Eastern Europe. The Dahman-Keusen family hated him. At that moment, I knew that I wouldn't be staying with them much longer.

But there were other, more positive aspects of my time in Mehlem. The Dahmann-Keusens introduced me to the music community in Bonn, and Frau Dahmann-Keusen and I regularly performed duets in house concerts for the couple's friends. A few weeks before I was to move out, Frau Dahman-Keusen asked if I might be able to teach a cello student for whom she did not have space. His name was Juergen von Schönfeld, and he was fifteen. He lived on the opposite side of Bad Godesburg from Mehlem, so for the next six months, I made the half-hour train ride back and forth to his home. At Yale, I'd worked as an assistant to Professor Parisot, so I had no problem teaching teenagers. But I had never taught cello lessons in German.

Juergen was a pleasant young man who could have been a model for one of the Hummel figurines. Initially, he was quite tentative when speaking to me, and seemed uncomfortable during our lessons. However, after a few visits we developed a rapport. His mother was always hospitable, and many afternoons after Juergen's lesson she would serve me coffee and cake in her parlor. We had lengthy conversations about German politics and the plight of East Germans, including her family, who had been forced to flee their homes after the Nazis confiscated most of their possessions. The von Schönfelds were descendants of nobility, and until the early twentieth century when monarchies were abolished, the family had been considered a special class of citizens with special rights and privileges. After 1919, however, the "von" simply became an ordinary part of their name in Germany; in Austria, it was eliminated altogether.

While there was little difference between my interactions with the Dahmann-Keusens and the von Schönfelds, there was a huge contrast in the way their homes were appointed. The Dahmann-Keusen household was quite modern, and the von Schönfelds' was filled with family heirlooms and antiques. They were from two distinctly different classes, and it fascinated me.

After six months, Frau Dahmann-Keusen asked me to bring Juergen to play for her. The request caught me by surprise, so I was a bit nervous. I told Juergen to play a sonata that he'd studied with me, as well as an étude. Apparently, Frau Dahmann-Keusen was impressed, because soon after, I received an offer to teach at the Bonn Music School.

By then, I was ready to leave the Dahmann-Keusens. But finding a new place to live that would allow me to practice cello in the early mornings, as I preferred, was difficult. (To this day, I rise early and play for an hour every day at six a.m.) In frustration, I gave up on the Fulbright organizers and asked the woman coordinating the Experiment in International Living if she knew of any rooms for rent in Bonn or Bad Godesberg. Soon after, I was ringing the doorbell of the Petri family on Paracel-susstrasse in Lannesdorf, a suburb of Bad Godesberg. Mrs. Petri and her youngest son, Martin, invited me in.

Suzanne Petri had been born in Wisconsin, and she mostly spoke English to her four boys. But she'd majored in German at the University of Wisconsin–Madison and met her husband, Hans-Werner, during a year of study abroad in Germany. As a dual citizen of both countries, Suzanne wanted all four of her sons to be able to speak English fluently. And she wanted them to be comfortable with all kinds of people. Over the years they'd hosted visitors and renters from all around the world. Mrs. Petri kept a guest book filled with comments and momentos from each of the guests who had stayed with her family. From the Petris' example, I learned a great deal about the benefits of cross-cultural exchange.

Their home was a three-story row house at the very end of a residential street lined with other row houses and apartment buildings. It sat next to a footway that led to the town's main thoroughfare, Deutschherrenstrasse. My room was on the top floor, adjacent to the bedroom where two of Suzanne's sons slept. Through my dormer window, I had stunning views of the famous Siebenge-birge (Seven Hills) mountain range, on top of which perched the famous Hotel Petersberg, seat of the Allied High Commission for Germany during WWII.

My early morning practice habits were no problem for the Petris since they were all up by five a.m. They treated me like a member of the family, throwing my laundry into a pile with the other boys' clothes and observing my birthday in February, right along with three of their sons'. But they also allowed me privacy. I spent many hours exploring Bonn and Cologne on my own, and because I was trying to save my money for travel, I ate most meals alone in my room. I found that I rather enjoyed this solitude. It provided lots of time for me to think.

Hans-Werner Petri was a wine collector, and he and his wife often invited me downstairs for a glass at the end of the day. We would talk about politics, history, and what life was like in the United States for Black people. After I had been with them for a few months, Hans-Werner mentioned that he had joined the Hitler Youth as a boy, then quit when he realized just what kinds of beliefs the organization was teaching its recruits. More than thirty years later, he was still wracked with guilt, sometimes nearly to the point of tears. I'd learned quite a bit about Jews and Judiaism as a child in Cincinnati. Rockdale Temple, one of the oldest and largest in the city, was located two blocks from our home. My father had taught us that Judaism was different from Christianity, with their sabbath that ran from sundown on Friday until sunset on Saturday. But as I watched the families walking by our home to celelbrate the High Holy Days at Rockdale Temple, I kept thinking how similar they looked to families attending our Zion Baptist Church, except for the color of their skin. Now, alone in my room at the Petris, I pondered what Hans-Werner had told me. I wondered if there were parallels to young people in America who'd joined the

Ku Klux Klan. I could see how it might feel seductive to be embraced by a group, and how easily a young person might be duped.

The Petris also belonged to an organization comprised of other German-American couples called the German-American Friends, and they always invited me to join them when they were hosting the group. Almost all of these couples had met during some kind of study abroad experience, and I was fascinated to hear about the adjustments necessary in navigating cross-cultural relationships. Some parents insisted that their children be immersed solely in German culture; others wanted to create more ease with both. I learned a great deal about the importance of compromise in loving relationships from these interactions. The Petris were becoming almost like a second set of parents to me. I lived with them for three years.

Ron at the Petris, 1974

Through my letters home, my own parents learned to love the Petris too. Mainly, out of gratitude. My mother came to feel so warmly toward my adopted family that she knitted them six wool caps, one for each member of the Petri clan. Forty years later, Sue Petri still had them, carefully folded. When I visited in 2017, she pulled each one out of storage, transporting me backward to another time. The Petri boys had written thank-you notes to my mother, and my father saved them just as Sue had saved my mother's knit caps. Sometimes the smallest trinkets hold enormous powers for reconnecting us to ourselves.

At the time, administrative organization was not a strong suit in German institutions of higher learning. When I traveled to Cologne to register at the State Academy of Music, I was told that I needed two passport-size photographs. I showed the registrar the papers that had been sent to me by the school, none of which made any mention of bringing photos.

"Everyone knows that you have to have these photos in order to register," the registrar replied curtly.

I finally lost it. Maybe it was the ongoing tension around being a foreigner. Maybe all of the logistical struggles around finding housing. Maybe I felt it was because of the color of my skin. Whatever had triggered me, I started screaming at the woman in German. Her face turned red, and she became visibly nervous. Voice shaking, the registrar told me where I could get photos made, then allowed me to cut the line in front of several other students when I returned with the pictures. (In a rule-bound culture like Germany in those days, such line-cutting was unusual indeed.) Several weeks later while walking into the school cafeteria, I ran into her. "Guten Tag, Herr Crutcher," she said politely. My friends were amazed. The registrar never spoke to students, they said. Perhaps showing my frustration had actually been useful.

I was taking musicology classes at the Friedrich-Wilhelms-Universität in Bonn and studying cello forty-five minutes away in Cologne. As with many of my experiences in Germany, my studies got off to a rocky start. For acceptance into Siegfried Palm's class, I'd performed the first movement of the Dvorak Concerto in B Minor. When I finished he snorted, "Typisch Amerikanisch, alle Tecknik und keine Musik!" (Typical American, all technique and no music.) It stung. But after a few months of studying with Professor Palm, I knew I wanted to continue with him for at least another year. Everything about my plans was changing.

My intention in Germany had been to study contemporary works for cello. But under Professor Palm I was instead filling gaps in my knowledge of the canon. It was his approach—with a focus on musicality, rather than technique—that felt groundbreaking. I found myself paying attention to the phrasing and contour of each piece. This was a revelation. It certainly made me a better musician. But to get more time with Professor Palm, I would need to extend my fellowship, and everyone told me this was virtually impossible. I applied for an extension anyway.

In the meantime, I received a job offer from Carleton College as an instructor in music. Before leaving the US, I'd interviewed for a teaching position at Carleton, and the school sent me an official offer letter just about the time that I applied for an extension. I signed the contract with Carleton to teach music for an annual salary of eleven thousand dollars—anticipating that my extension would never pan out—and prepared to return to the US the following fall. In less than a month, I received word that my extension had been granted.

This embarrassment of riches inspired in me panic rather than joy. I simply could not figure out which path to take. In the end, I wrote a letter to Carleton's president, Howard Swearer, thanking him for the offer and explaining the significance of my Fulbright extension. It was excruciating. With abject apologies, I asked to have my contract rescinded. But President Swearer was understanding. The position would be there for me when I returned in a year, he promised. In the end, I remained in Germany for longer than either of us anticipated—almost five years.

My developing sense of self meant being a cellist who had his own approach to the instrument and to interpreting the music of the masters. But that necessitated a delicate tightrope walk. I wanted my performances to be recognized for their virtuosity and musicality. But my being Black created tension for some of my German listeners. All was fine during my debut recitals in Brussels and Bonn, where reviewers praised my interpretations and only mentioned my Blackness as an aside. But often, while the German people welcomed me as a musician and scholar, music critics constantly brought up my race, describing me as the "colored cellist." I doubt that these mentions were intended to slight my performances, though I interpreted them that way at the time. For years, I smarted at the sense that reviewers didn't know what to make of me as a classical musician.

This cacophony of praise mixed with subtle racism was exasperating. I wondered if I would ever be recognized solely as a musician. My German friends tried to calm me. They urged me to ignore the critics. But it was nearly impossible. I wanted to be accepted within the German intelligentsia as an artist, not as a "colored" artist, and these reviewers were the gatekeepers. The tension never resolved completely, and it eventually prompted my return to the United States.

However, things did not necessarily improve in the United States. Throughout my career, I have found myself explaining why and how it was that I, first, became a professional classical musician and, then, how I became a leader in higher education. Even as late as 1990, when I was vice president for Academic Affairs and dean of the conservatory at the Cleveland Institute of Music, I recall an uncomfortable evening of conversation at a dinner hosted by one of my former colleagues from Yale. He was by then a professor at Case Western Reserve University, and he and his wife invited me to their home, along with two musicians from the Cleveland Orchestra. One of them was a cellist. I spent the entire evening trying to explain to these two musicians why I was qualified for my position. The same old firing squad of questions I'd fended off all my life. In situations like this, I tend to proceed calmly, quietly sharing my background, then accelerating to add more and more information. I call it the cobra effect. It starts with an easy, nonthreatening charm, then I strike. My greatest pleasure is when people walk away charmed, buoyed, and one step closer to questioning their assumptions.

My decision to stay in Germany was nothing I could have envisioned at the outset of my adventure, when I noticed people staring at me every day. But the change happened relatively fast. After living abroad for six months, I realized how pleasant it was not to constantly feel the need to explain my decision to become a musician. On the contrary, in Germany musicians were revered. The parents of my students at the Bonn Music School treated me like royalty, often inviting me into their homes for dinner and presenting me with lavish gifts at Chritsmas or on my birthday. I loved the way Germans took time to enjoy each other during meals; they did not bolt their food, as is so often the case in American homes. I loved the sight of aging German hikers in their seventies and eighties, who left me in the dust when I walked in the Seven Hills.

Most of all, aside from my frustrations with music reviewers, in Germany I rarely thought about race. This surprised me. But it was only when I stepped away from life in the US that I realized how much energy that topic had consumed. As a student, I'd spent an inordinate amount of time thinking about how people—particularly white people—were going to react to me. It was exhausting. In Germany, by contrast, I felt unencumbered. Other than those strange moments with the waitress at Hotel zum Löwen and Herr Dahmann-Keusen, race hardly came up with my colleagues and friends there. Many confided that they did not think of me as American; I spoke their language, and had adapted to the European lifestyle. I was a citizen of the world now, and I'd never felt so free.

While studying in Cologne and Bonn, I made my European debut as a solo cellist, performing with an American pianist. One concert, booked for a hall in Brussels, was scheduled for October 22, 1973—the day Pablo Casals passed away. I heard the announcement on the US Armed Forces radio station, and my heart sank. I would perform my first solo recital in Europe on the day when the world's greatest living cellist had died—was there a message in this? It worried me. The pianist and I drove from Bonn to Brussels that afternoon, transporting a harpsichord, which we needed for our first piece, the Bach Sonata for Cello and Harpsichord. But at the Belgian border we were stopped. "Do you have proof that this instrument is yours?" the officers demanded. My pianist nervously offered his papers and made a phone call to the harpsichord's manufacturer. We were allowed, finally, to cross. But the delay made us two hours late to the concert hall. There was still time before we were to go on stage, but I was a wreck. I need to be composed when I perform, with a calm, internal focus, and here I was worried about passports and papers and border guards. But our host provided a quiet room for each of us, and I was able to meditate briefly before the recital. We received a glowing review.

Our Bonn debut was scheduled very soon after at the famed Hotel Dreesen. I'd hoped to perform at Redoute Hall, where Beethoven is said to have played for Haydn as a boy. But the Redoute was being renovated, so we were moved to the Dreesen, where Adolf Hitler and Neville Chamberlain met to work out the disastrous Munich Agreement of 1938, a summit now synonymous with the futility of appeasing a totalitarian state.

I had a very active musical life in Bonn, performing often with a number of esteemed artists, including pianists Heide von Dreising and Alyce LeBlanc, the late violinist Lynn Blakeslee, and clarinetist Michael Neuhalfen. The longer I lived there, the more involved I became in Germany's classical music scene. I performed in every kind of venue from grand halls to humble homes, and served as the principal cellist of the Kur Kölnishes chamber orchestra, giving concerts throughout the state of North Rhine-Westfalia.

Simultaneously, my social life was deepening. I'd made many friends among the college students participating in the Experiment in International Living and developed a real bond with Albert Brancato, a graduate student from Philadelphia. He'd had come to Germany to work on a dissertation about the "Anschluss" (annexation) of Austria into Nazi Germany. Most weekends, we traveled together. Once, at Christmas, we visited Albert's Italian relatives in a small town near Salerno. They treated us like visiting dignitaries, inviting us to sit at the altar with the town priest for Christmas Eve services. Dinner on Christmas Day was a nine-course meal. I had never eaten so much in my entire life. Nor have I since.

One evening, as I waited for Albert to pick me up on the way to a party, I began reading Thomas Mann's classic novel, *Buddenbrooks*. Albert was late. When ten minutes became twenty and then thirty, I walked over to the mirror and stared at my reflection. *If Albert doesn't show, what's the worst that can happen?* I asked myself. The answer: I would continue reading a great book, and I would be fine. It was the first moment that I consciously understood what it means to be alone without feeling lonely. After that, I knew I could be at home pretty much anywhere.

I'd become so comfortable in Germany that the thought of leaving tore me apart. I kept my return ticket to the US on hold for four years, unable to commit. I knew how transformative this experience had been. I'd arrived as a young man, hyperconscious about my race, and feeling that it separated me from everyone. Five years later, I felt more European than American, and for the first time in my life race no longer dominated my psyche. Living abroad also provided me with an unexpected vantage point on the uglier realities of life in the United States. At one point, I became so enamored of this world where musicians were revered and Blacks were not ostracized that I considered never returning to the US at all.

But as my thirtieth birthday approached, I began to think seriously about what kind of future I wanted. I knew a family would be part of it, and the thought of raising children in a place where they would be removed from their roots as Black Americans left me cold. For more than sixty years, my mother's family had held reunions each July—would I want my children to miss out on this rich tradition? I couldn't bear the thought. I didn't want my family and their ways to seem foreign. I didn't want to explain strange-sounding accents. America was my country, warts and all. No matter how comfortable I felt in this unexpected second home, I was American, and I wanted my future children to have an authentic American experience as well.

I made my decision one day in mid-August, though I kept half of my belongings in the Petris' attic, just in case. A week later, my cello and I boarded a Lufthansa flight back to America. My first six months home were rough. Weekly, I had to fight the urge to get on a plane and fly back to Germany. Where was home, really? There were so many things about American culture that bothered me. Highways overwhelmed with billboards blocking out the mountains and trees offended my eyes. At Christmas-time, I went shopping with my younger brother, staring in disgust at displays filled with cheap merchandise. For a moment I felt a nearly uncontrollable urge to flip the tables, like Jesus in the temple. I was so agitated that I had to sit in the car while my brother continued browsing. And then there was American television. I didn't own a TV set, having refused to purchase one, but my parents presented me with a small black and white portable as a Christmas gift. I felt like the commercials were trying to brainwash me. Why couldn't America do as the Germans did and bundle these spots together at the end of a show, rather than interrupting the program? None of it made sense to me. All of it grated.

Eventually, I reconciled myself to living in the United States, and Germany came to feel like a second home. I know my experience there helped me come to terms with what W. E. B. DuBois called the "double consciousness" of the African-American. As a result, I no longer suffer the trauma of seeing myself through the eyes of a racist society. Rather, I am proud of the capabilities that have helped me to persevere in spite of challenges.

To put it plainly, Germany helped me reach the highest level on Maslow's hierarchy of needs: self-actualization. I needed to leave America to do it. But there is no doubt in my mind learning how to be alone was the catalyst. Without Germany, I would not be the American I am today.

Chapter Nine:
The Vision Can be Real

Studies show that first-generation and less-advantaged students are the ones most likely to enroll in narrowly focused, technical training schools. This should not be surprising in today's climate where so much emphasis is placed on the cost of higher education and the difficulty that some graduates of high-priced institutions have in finding jobs upon graduation. The public is bombarded by advertisements from community colleges and propri-etary institutions about the success their own graduates have in building careers. It concerns me, because young people who come from less-advantaged backgrounds are precisely the ones who can benefit most from the kind of critical thinking and communication skills that form the foundation of a liberal arts education.

This segmenting—or tracking of students into differ-ent programs with very different expectations—has deep roots, and I've altered my thinking about it over the years. Once, I was a supporter. Indeed, I benefitted from academic tracking in elementary school, and I was stung when that honors-style acceleration was suddenly stripped away. But in later years, shaped by the experiences of my wife, Betty, and our daughter, Sara, I have become more aware of how fickle and damaging the practice can be, especially for the young.

Betty and I met on a blind date in Detroit, in 1979. We were introduced (or set up) by a mutual friend whom I had known at Yale during graduate school. Actually, I'd met Linda Stokes Smith in high school, but I didn't get to know her until we both found ourselves at Yale as grad students. When I returned home from Germany in 1977, having lived overseas for almost five years, Linda invited me to Detroit to meet her husband and son. I had visited the city often as a child. In fact, the first trip I ever made without my parents was a train ride to Detroit with my maternal grandmother, Mama Katie. Her oldest son, my Uncle Charles, had done maintenance on planes flown by the Tuskegee Airmen in Alabama, and along the way he'd learned how to fly them too. Uncle Charles owned a Piper Cub, and he took my brother Larry and me up into the sky for a flight, at one point opening his window to extend a handkerchief into the open air. When he brought it back inside, the handkerchief was in shreds. This terrified me, but as usual I kept quiet.

I loved Detroit, but didn't want to visit Linda until I was done with my doctoral studies. (You'll recall that the prospect of oral exams on music history and theory had been so daunting that I considered giving up.) The day that I finally passed, January 26, 1979, I called Linda from New Haven.

She set Betty and me up to have dinner. But Linda was so worried that I might bring her friend to a cheap restaurant that she cooked us a meal herself. Betty dropped by a few hours early to check in about something else, and Linda called me to the door to meet her. I was wearing bell-bottoms with suspenders over a t-shirt, and Betty looked less than impressed. But by the appointed hour, I had dressed in a new sport coat and cleaned up considerably. I walked into Linda's sunken living room to reintroduce myself, and Betty raised her hand, firmly telling me to back off. "Not now," she said. "I'm meditating."

A few minutes later we finally sat down in Linda's kitchen. By the end of the meal, I felt as if I had known Betty for years. She suggested that we head downtown to the Renaissance Center, a grand new riverfront complex and promenade. I was feeling so good that I suggested we stop by my Uncle Chester's house on the way. Just as I was about to ring his doorbell with Betty at my side, my mind went blank. I'd completely forgotten her name. (Nerves will do that.) Betty graciously glided past this awkwardness, which impressed me all over again.

As Betty remembers it, I interrogated her during our drive through the city. I asked about her education and goals. What were her aspirations? A doctoral degree in social work, and then she'd become the Secretary of Health, Education, and Welfare, Betty said. *Wow*, I

thought. *She's more than just pretty.* I was soon sharing my
entire life story with this woman I had known for merely
hours. We talked so much that we were late for Betty's ten
p.m. curfew. Then we sat outside the hall where she was to
attend a fraternity event and continued our conversation,
parked in my car. When she finally stepped out, I knew
Betty Neal was the woman I wanted to marry.

Of course, I wanted her to meet my family and close
friends. At the time I was living in Springfield, Ohio, and
working as an assistant professor of music at Wittenberg
University, where I'd been appointed to develop a string
program. We planned a visit to my parents' weekend
getaway on the Ohio River to celebrate Mother's Day.
Several of the Klemperers and Liz Potteiger would be
there too. Betty bought a beautiful plant for my mother,
though my cat ate it and later peed all over my journals
and magazines arrayed on the floor of my apartment, as I
had no bookcases. I put thousands of miles on my Datsun
that spring of 1979, traveling back and forth between
Springfield and Detroit, to visit with Betty and drive her
all over the Midwest meeting my relatives and friends.
Three months after our first evening together, I proposed
at Hueston Woods State Park, and on November 24,
1979, about eight months after we first met, Betty and
I were married at Oak Grove AME Church in Detroit.

During our counseling sessions beforehand, the pastor
had asked us what Betty and I would do if we were unable
to conceive, or as the pastor put it, "if the dog has no
teeth." We agreed that we would adopt. When it became

apparent after several medical investigations that our only option was in vitro fertilization, we immediately began adoption proceedings.

About a year later, in November of 1984, the Children's Home Society called. They had matched us with a little girl. Sara was six weeks old when we met her, and I will never forget the way her face broke into a huge smile when she looked at us. Incredibly, she bore a striking resemblance to my mother.

I took a six-week leave of absence from my post as associate principal cello of the Greensboro Symphony Orchestra to stay home with Sara at the beginning. When she was nine months old, we enrolled her in a child care center on the University of North Carolina–Greensboro campus, within walking distance from my office in the music building. Every day just before noon I would walk down to McIver Street to have lunch with my baby girl. Every day, Sara stood at the window, waiting, and would not eat until I'd arrived.

But well before Sara celebrated her first birthday, it was apparent that something was amiss. At first it seemed like she had trouble paying attention. I ignored this and just kept reading to her. When she was about four, a teacher at McIver Child Care recommended that she take a test, the Wechsler Preschool & Primary Scale of Intelligence. It showed that while she ranked high intellectually, Sara's difficulty in maintaining attention warranted serious evaluation. I vividly recall discussing this with Betty and insisting that the most important thing was Sara's intellectual score—the 90th percentile. In my opinion, that was the only result that mattered: Sara had been proven highly intelligent. I remained clueless about the impact of her disability and how it would affect her learning. In retrospect, it's clear that we should have taken her to a pediatric psychologist for further evaluation. Two years later, when Sara was almost six and we were living in Cleveland, her pediatrician raised the same issue. This time, we brought Sara to a psychologist, who diagnosed her with Attention Deficit Disorder. But it was another four years of rotating medications before we finally learned that our daughter also had an auditory processing disorder that prevented her from understanding aural cues the same way that other kids do. This hearing problem affects some 5% of school-aged children, and it can be caused by something as ordinary as chronic ear infections (as well as head trauma or lead poisoning). Sara had suffered many ear infections as a baby, and getting her correctly diagnosed was an absolute game-changer. We were living in Austin, Texas, by then, and we set her up with a speech language pathologist who prescribed a milder medication for Sara's ADHD. Within a few months, and some hard work on auditory processing, my daughter's reading was immensely improved.

Watching her struggle in school had been a real wake-up call for me. Sara had often insisted that she "didn't like" to read. Yet we could see how bright she was. It was terribly confusing. Once she was diagnosed and treated correctly, Sara's life as a student transformed. Betty and I understood that only because of our positions in academia—what we would now call privilege—were we able to get our daughter the help she needed. That experience upended all of my beliefs about what children can do and how we impede them by dictating too early who gets fast-tracked and who does not.

All of this happened shortly before I became president at Wheaton College, which was trying mightily to grapple with these kinds of issues, while diversifying its faculty and student body. Diversify, we did. But along the way, it became clear that the process requires a lot more than simply tweaking demographics.

The difficulties of diversity became apparent even before I took the position.

I'd applied for the job, spoken with the search committee and made a good impression, I thought. The executive search consultant confirmed this. But now, oddly, I was being asked back for another round of interviews. "They want to know who the real Ron Crutcher is," the consultant told me. "As a Black man, you're shrouded in question marks—is he really this good? Just be real," the consultant advised. "Be authentic. Be yourself."

I was floored. I am often described as overly formal—perhaps because my mother taught my brothers and me that as Black boys we needed to watch ourselves every minute; we could never completely let loose. Otherwise, mother feared, people would stereotype us. Throughout my childhood, we'd been instructed to speak a certain way, dress just so, and act like mini-adults. Now it felt like I was being scrutinized precisely because I'd followed those rules. But I resolved to try and loosen up a bit.

After my second round of interviews at Wheaton, the search consultant got back to me. "What did you say to those people—they loved you!" he crowed.

Well, I hadn't been "authentic," exactly. I'd simply paused before responding to their questions, rather than reacting out of impatience or emotion—just as I had years before with the Texas oil magnate who'd been so shocked to discover my race. This practice of holding my tongue and waiting a beat before responding is one I've cultivated all my life. I believe it forces me to listen more deeply, and often I learn something. But it's a habit of mind I see less and less often—especially on college campuses.

When I became a finalist for the job at Wheaton, no one mentioned my race to the Board of Trustees. Nor did most of the newspapers when I was named to the position. And so I tried not to make much of the fact that I was Wheaton's first Black president—not initially. I was soon to learn, however, that my race did indeed make a difference, even at a bastion of liberalism like Wheaton.

It first showed up merely as a culture clash. My predecessor, who had always been addressed by her first name, instructed the staff to refer to me as President Crutcher. This was the norm on historically Black college campuses, she'd told them, trying, I think, to ease my entry. And it is true that I am fairly formal when first meeting people. As a little boy, it had always bothered me that white people in town called my grandfather "Andy," while he addressed them as "Mr." When I grow up, I told myself, no one would call me by my first name without my permission.

I was soon to learn that my childhood sensitivity to the hierarchies implied by forms of address was one with deep historical roots. During the years I led Wheaton, Betty and I were regular New Year's Day guests at the home of the writer and activist Maya Angelou. We'd met her initially through friends in North Carolina. And I recall sitting on the sofa in their living room when a booming voice thundered through the house. "Where is the cellist? I want to meet the cellist!" Dr. Angelou said as she stepped through the front door. Before I knew it, she was standing above me, looking down. In personal style, we were not much alike. But Dr. Angelou and I forged an abiding friendship based on our shared love of the arts. By 2004, when I started at Wheaton, Betty and I came to anticipate our New Year's Day brunches at Dr. Angelou's home in Harlem with excitement—in part beause there were always so many interesting guests to talk with. Cicely Tyson was usually there, as well as the writer and activist Louise Meriweather, and James Baldwin's sister-in-law Helen. The menu—all soul food—was always incredible. But even more memorable were Dr. Angelou's rules about the way her guests were to address the kitchen staff: always with proper honorifics. In the South, she explained, Black servants had been referred to by first names only, which in her opinion was disrespectful. In her household, Dr.

Angelou would make sure that every person was treated with respect.

I was similarly attuned to these signals. As a result, I had always been careful to tell colleagues how I preferred to be addressed. At Wheaton, I asked that the faculty call me Ron, but I wanted the staff to refer to me as Dr. Crutcher or President Crutcher until we knew each other better. This caused an absolute firestorm among the female professors. If the staff could not call me "Ron," they wouldn't either. But not one of them had the courage to tell me to my face. I was informed by a group of Black male professors. Even then, I didn't fully understand the minefield I was walking through. While I'd shrugged off the awkwardness, my male colleagues explained that the women were trying to teach me a lesson. Did it really stem from heartfelt solidarity with lower-tier staff? I was never entirely certain.

My next misstep was appointing an outsider as my special assistant. When I arrived at Wheaton, there was no one in the Office of the President charged with handling my communications. I thought it was critically important to have a senior-level professional in that role, so I hired someone with deep experience who'd been recommended to me by a search-consultant friend. While my assistant's skills were indeed exceptional, women in the office found him intimidating. I'd explained that I wanted faculty, in particular, to have direct access to me. But he interpreted his role as more of a gatekeeper. Nine months into my presidency, a group of Black colleagues again called me to a meeting to share their concerns. They felt this assistant was purposely trying to undermine my leadership. And it was working with the white faculty, who assumed that I'd endorsed his high-handed style.

All of this behind-the-back whispering and crossed communication came to a head as I was working on my inaugural speech in April 2005, nine months after taking office. I knew this event would bring more Black people to Wheaton's campus than the college had ever seen, and I was a bit worried about the reaction from alumni and the wider Norton, Massachusetts, community. My father had chartered a bus full of relatives and church members from Cincinnati. Many other friends would be coming from across the country. Betty alerted the Chief of Police when we ran into him at the dry cleaners in town, asking him to refrain from arresting anyone who might look "different." He smiled, and assured us there was no need to worry, but he appeared startled by her remark.

It was a difficult time, marked by mutual mistrust between the faculty and me. When I finally announced that my special assistant would no longer be handling daily in-office duties, the relief was palpable. But it irritated me that no white faculty had made the effort to reach across the divide and talk these problems through. As the college's first Black president, I'd never expected the white faculty to immediately embrace me as one of their own. But I did expect a show of basic respect.

Mine was indeed an inauguration unlike any other in the history of Wheaton College. My father sat in the first row, surrounded by a sea of Black faces. They dominated the entire front section of the fieldhouse. As I approached the stage, I noticed that almost all the male faculty were wearing bow ties, apparently in a gesture of solidarity with my signature style. The sight moved me almost as much as all the familiar faces from home. The instant I finished speaking, my father leaped to his feet, applauding madly. For years to come, whenever my dad visited me at Wheaton he'd walk the campus each morning, march up to anyone he saw, and stick out his hand. "I'm A. J. Crutcher Jr., President Crutcher's father," he'd say, so proud he might burst.

I daresay no president at lily-white Wheaton had ever organized an after-party like mine, either. The all-Black a cappella group Sweet Honey in the Rock sang "We Who Believe in Freedom Shall Not Rest," a song inspired by the words of Ella Baker. The following evening, they performed in the chapel before a packed house. But not everyone was pleased. A month later, Betty and I were lunching with a Wheaton alumna and her husband at the Harvard Club in Boston. How wonderful it had been to march into the fieldhouse and see so many Black people, she told Betty. "Do you think other alumni felt the same?" my wife asked pointedly. The woman, looking very embarrassed, admitted that many had not been happy about the overwhelming number of Blacks on campus that day. "I guess we're not quite as liberal as we think we are," she said.

Early in my tenure, I spoke with the faculty about diversifying their ranks. Students of color had challenged Wheaton's teachers to do exactly that, mirroring the school's effort to make its student body more inclusive. Wheaton had gone about that work through a partnership with the Posse Foundation, which identifies high-achieving inner-city high school graduates and places them in cohorts of ten (a "Posse") at colleges and universities. At Wheaton, it markedly increased the number of students of color in a very short time frame. But when students asked for comparable changes in the faculty, they were told there were no Black applicants with the requisite skills and experience. (The old "limited pool of appropriate candidates" excuse.) The students would have none of it, challenging their teachers to do better. And they did. In June 2000, the *Chronicle of Higher Education* noted that 50% of new tenure-track hires at Wheaton were Black. "Wheaton says it shows determination and luck; critics wonder if race played too large a role," the article began. Almost immediately, a Wheaton professor wrote a scathing confirmation of that criticism, asserting that the college had hired Black faculty who were less qualified than its white candidates.

This dispute points at the heart of my difficulties with affirmative action. While I have undoubtedly benefitted from the practice—the Ford Foundation scholarship that paid for my tuition, books, and fees at Yale was an affirmative action program aimed at getting more Blacks into higher education teaching jobs—I have seen it turned into a weapon undercutting the very people it was meant to lift up. In fact, from the moment President Kennedy first used the term, affirmative action has been perceived by whites as a means for giving an advantage to people assumed to be less qualified. For this reason, despite its original intent—and onetime necessity—affirmative action has not served Black and brown people well. The result is that we are often called to justify why we are "qualified" for certain positions. That goes for me too, even after years of working in the upper echelons of higher education. It never becomes easier to swallow.

The Ford Foundation Fellowship was the first time in my life that I knew I'd received an exceptional benefit as a result of being a talented Black man. I later learned that the alumni merit scholarship allowing me to attend Miami University came as a result of Liz Potteiger bequeathing it on me rather than my old friend Leon Friedberg. Purportedly, it was a scholarship to recognize talent. Did the fact that I was Black also enter into Liz's calculations? I will never know.

As the president at Wheaton, I explained to the faculty that my goals for diversity went beyond "social justice." In the sixties, we'd naively believed that opening up institutions to "unknown brothers and sisters" would magically change the culture. We have learned through bitter experience how wrong that is. The problem that bedevils any organization seeking to make these changes is that they rarely devote much thought to helping people see the end game. What will the culture of the institution be like if it becomes more diverse? Will it be the same place, just with more Black, brown, or yellow faces? Or will it be fundamentally different? This is why colleges and universities must act deliberately when using diversity to create culture change. It's rarely smooth, but I believe, in the end, that the rewards are worth some discomfort. Truly functioning diversity is an educational asset central to the intellectual mission of a college. That was why we needed to ingrain it in the very fabric of our campus community, I explained at Wheaton, rather than merely trying to satisfy some sort of demographic quotient. I was convinced that if we could make it work as intended, diversity would bring about a culture change benefitting everyone.

But changing mindsets is not an easy thing to do. How does one train another human being in matters of the heart? I have never been a great fan of diversity training programs because I believe you cannot change a person's perceptions about others without first changing their heart. In other words, attempting to drag people to a new worldview by forcing them to understand white privilege or microaggressions (a term that I abhor) is a waste of time, in my opinion. Some research shows that it can actually make matters worse.

In my experience, intergroup dialog is the best pathway toward changing hearts and thus deepening a collective understanding of the impact of racism on daily life in America. The University of Michigan began using this method in 2003, in the wake of the controversial Grutter v. Bollinger case, which upheld affirmative action in college admissions. The overriding aim of these conversations is to help people from different backgrounds build mutual trust and respect through an authentic exchange. At Wheaton, we brought two consultants to campus to help us position diversity as educational benefit. They introduced the concept of intergroup dialog, and we developed small teams of eight to twelve people—some all-student, others comprised of faculty and staff—that would meet for five sessions to discuss a specific problem. For example, the intersection of race, class, gender, and technology on college campuses. Then each team developed recommendations for addressing it.

My group wanted to tackle the intersection of race and class. At first, each of us described our background and upbringing. Then came our first group exercise. It was designed to point out the advantages and disadvantages each member had experienced based on their race and class (whether or not our parents had a college education, for example; or owned their own home; or owned more than one home). Wheaton could not call itself a skilled intercultural community until every person on campus felt they had the capacity to engage authentically across race, class, and ideological divides. I saw the effects after just two sessions. The members of my group became increasingly comfortable with one another, and we were able to have very open conversations. The end goal was to turn all these discussions into incubators for concrete action. Though the Great Recession forced me to make cuts to the staff and facilitators, significantly hindering our efforts,

Wheaton pressed ahead, organizing a series of luncheons to achieve the same end. (The first of these gatherings was titled "Oriental is a Rug.")

I believe similar conversations would be useful for everyone in our democracy, college students or not.

Chapter Ten:
Spiral Up

FOR ME AS a college president, move-in day means pulling on a pair of shorts with a polo shirt to help students lug suitcases and furniture into their dorm rooms. Betty and I did this at Wheaton College for ten years. We've continued the practice at Richmond, and often students and their families have no idea who we are. (We don't wear name tags or any other identifiers.) This has led to some interesting experiences.

During my second year leading Richmond, I walked into a room where a mother and daughter were unpacking, and asked if they needed any help. I did not introduce myself. The mother answered that they were waiting for her husband to return with some tools to fix the small refrigerator that they had brought with them. While our conversation was pleasant, it was clear that this woman assumed I was one of the student development staff members. That evening, as I walked to the podium to welcome the incoming class, I noticed her excitedly nudging her husband. "That's the man who walked into our room this morning!" she exclaimed.

In this way, I've gathered a tremendous amount of intelligence about what motivates families to spend hundreds of thousands of dollars on private colleges and universities for their children. I learn what they're looking for and sometimes what they fear. It's important to hear these views unfiltered, and they've had a powerful impact on the way I lead. What I've seen is that the value proposition of higher education has assumed a much more prominent role in the past five years. Research from Richmond's marketing office confirms this. Parents expect that we will provide multiple opportunities for their children to connect academic interests with a vocation. Unspoken, but blazingly clear, is the message that they expect students either to have a job or be headed to graduate school upon graduation. Yet I lead a liberal arts institution, not a professional training school. So I rarely speak about liberal arts education as an end in itelf, but rather as a *means* to an end, a vehicle for helping students connect their academic interests to the real world.

There are other college presidents who have been professional musicians—among them, Leon Botstein at Bard, and my mentor the late Bryce Jordan, formerly of Penn State University. While these two men could not be more different, both have a musician's ear for close, active listening, something I believe is essential for enlightened leadership. Active listening is best described as the ability to hear various strains—whether dueling melodies or competing ideologies—while performing as part of a group. Obviously, this is a skill that's essential for any musician. But it applies to other pursuits as well. Active listening makes it possible for me to listen polyphonically—that is, hearing multiple conversations at once—when I attend cocktail parties or receptions. During a meeting or one-on-one conversation, it also allows me to listen to others while framing my own thoughts.

Botstein, famed for his eccentric, visionary zeal, embodies the conductor model of leadership, coordinating an orchestra of projects with frenzied energy—the man never stops thinking, moving, and innovating. He is utterly unafraid to take chances. By contrast, Jordan, who passed away in 2016, approached his role with an emphasis on collaboration and relationships, similar to the way a chamber ensemble works. Both were possessed of unwavering vision. And like all musicians who perform alongside others, both had an unerring ability to balance competing voices.

Business schools probably don't encourage their students to learn lessons in leadership from artists. But the fact is, all of the tools I've deployed successfully across my career in academic administration came through my pursuit of a career in music. My central focus in both realms is discord. In any musical composition, there may be a phrase that strikes the ear, initially, as somehow off. But if you stay with it, the harmonies eventually resolve. I feel similarly about leading institutions.

Unlike Botstein and Jordan, my primary experience in music has been as a performer in chamber trios and quartets. In these groups, decision-making is collaborative. But that should not imply mandatory consensus; if the group cannot agree on an interpretation, for instance, one player is designated to make the final call. Some ensembles rotate this responsibility, so that each player has the opportunity—really, the obligation—to lead. But most often the designated leader is a violinist because through creating melody, that instrument essentially leads listeners through a piece. The same is true when deciding on repertoire, a performance venue, or ensemble personnel. The hallmark of a good chamber ensemble is its seamlessness, the sense that each individual is contributing equally to the whole. Learning the value of this collaborative approach certainly helped me in academia. It taught me how to criticize thoughtfully, and also how to receive criticism from others—both essential leadership skills.

I developed these ideas—patience with discord, collaborative rigor, and an ability to balance competing voices—as a response to uncertainty and discomfort. And if I had to name my approach, I'd call it "spiraling up," a metaphor I conceived during my senior year at Miami University. I had prepared an essay for several national fellowship applications, reflecting on the puzzling fact that though I had accomplished all of the goals that I'd set for myself, I did not feel noticeably more confident as a college senior than I had as a first-year student. It happened again when I entered graduate school. Euphoric as I was about starting advanced studies at Yale, I had no more confidence then than I had as an eighteen-year-old freshman leaving home for the first time. This feeling of inadequacy haunted me. In New Haven, I was no longer a big fish in a small pond, as I'd felt by the time I left Oxford, Ohio. At Yale, I was just a nervous and insecure guppy among many big, confident bass. But slowly, I began to build relationships. I regularly attended Friday happy hours held in the Hall of Graduate Studies, making friends among students and faculty from Yale's law school, nursing school, medical school, forestry school, and the graduate school of arts and sciences. I attended a reception at the home of Yale's then-president Kingman Brewster, who remembered this and later greeting me by name when I ran into him on the street. Suddenly, I realized that I was walking the same ground I had when I enrolled at Miami. There is a déjà vu quality to our lives that I describe in visual terms. To me, life is much like climbing a spiral staircase. You continually circle over the same terrain, but at higher and higher levels. It may be a bit dizzying, but you build endurance with every upward step.

So it goes as we climb upwards in our careers. Everyone at times encounters situations that echo the past, and sometimes that feeling can be disheartening. But the fact is that through your own progression, you have accumulated more experience, more wisdom, and more confidence along with more wrinkles. This puts you in an infinitely stronger position to propel yourself forward—even if it feels like you're right back where you started.

The metaphor of spiraling up has helped me navigate many transitions in my career as a musician, teacher, and administrator. I've boiled it down to five principles that I consider essential for effective leadership, especially when navigating difference or discord:

Lesson One: *Develop a means of remaining focused (or centered, as the Quakers would call it), regardless of the situation.*

The principal ballerina Misty Copeland has said, "Find a Zen space in your mind, even if it's just singing to yourself. Just pass the time and keep a steady breath."

For some, remaining centered will mean meditating, for others prayer or some alternate form of contemplation. Exercise, particularly semi-solo pursuits like running, biking, working out, or yoga, are an excellent means of centering. My own routine has been unwavering for thirty-five years. I begin my day at five a.m. with twenty minutes of meditation. Afterward, I practice the cello, sometimes for only fifteen or twenty minutes, just to keep my fingers nimble. Then, at six a.m., Betty and I go to the gym. It may sound dull, but this pattern helps me remain focused throughout my day, and ensures a grounded center that keeps me steady when something out of the ordinary occurs. As the Latin scribe Publilius Syrus wrote back in the first century BC, "Anyone can hold a helm when the sea is calm." The challenge is to maintain your grip in a storm. Developing a means of remaining centered helps immeasurably, allowing calm, consistent performance under any kind of test.

This ability to remain steady under stress is imperative for anyone in leadership. During my five-year tenure as provost at Miami University, I invented an imaginary tool that I called the "S" shield. (You can probably guess what "S" stands for.) It was available to me at a moment's notice, and I always kept a hand on it, figuratively speaking, particularly at University Senate meetings. The shield could deflect acrimonious words. Mentally lifting it in front of my face was a reminder to remain centered if I found myself becoming agitated by the tenor of a discussion. It gave me time to breathe, listen closely, contemplate the precise nature of the statement, and respond appropriately.

It is true that I have not always had it at the ready, as during some of my tenser meetings with the faculty at Wheaton. After I'd been there five years and had been forced to institute a salary freeze, a professor stood up during a meeting and said I should have consulted with the faculty's Economic Status Committee before making that decision. I'd already taken a salary reduction myself, as had my vice presidents. I'd just learned that a friend's son had died young, and Betty—always a steadying force for me—was away, visiting the grieving family. I could feel the rage roiling my gut. This teacher was ignoring the fact that we'd already spent months in committee discussing various approaches to budget reduction—it was hardly a decision by fiat.

"That is utter bullshit and you know it," I said, looking straight at the teacher. It was all I could do to keep myself from lunging at him.

He sat down immediately. But one of his colleagues continued what felt to me like a public sabotage.

"Will you give me a fuckin' break!" I shouted. No one spoke for quite a few minutes. Finally, I explained what they knew full well, that the country was in the midst of a severe recession that would have serious financial repercussions for the college, and no one had time for playing games. Later that day, I received numerous emails from faculty colleagues thanking me for taking the stand that I had. "It's about time!" was the general gist. I interpreted their messages as confirmation that, while certainly out of character, my no-nonsense response had been necessary.

I was heartened by the support, but still disappointed with myself for losing control. There was no doubt that A. J. Crutcher Jr. was working through me that day. I offer this story to show that we can never take for granted the work of remaining centered. It is an ongoing practice.

Lesson Two: *Build an ethical foundation for the work you do.*

It cannot be primarily about money. I know all about the importance of solvency and fundraising and making a good salary. But I still say, if it's only about the money, you're probably in the wrong field. Consider Bill Gates or Oprah Winfrey—yes, each has amassed great fortunes.

But both were driven intially by the energy they had for the work itself, for discovery and communication.

Doing work for reasons beyond the financial becomes even more important if you begin to feel you are not paid enough—as nearly everyone does at some point. In *Life Work*, the poet and former University of Michigan professor Donald Hall describes the inseparability of his own life and work. "There are days, there are days," he writes. "The best day begins with waking early because I want so much to get out of bed and start working."

I, too, have had those best days when I can not wait to get up and play a particular piece, or continue researching a subject that has captured my fascination, or teach Gershwin's marvelous opera *Porgy and Bess* to an eager group of students. My life's work, and your life's work, cannot be solely about the money or, as is the case for many in the arts, lack thereof.

My passion for transforming the lives of students is a direct result of my own experience with my mentor and teacher Liz Potteiger; the gratification I feel witnessing transformation in others is my primary motivation. It is not necessary that every person feel intense passion for a job. But I believe we should all be able to answer the question "why do I do what I do?" with some response other than "for the fat paycheck" or "the prestige." Those answers, I promise, will eventually grow hollow. That is not to say money isn't important. It certainly is. But the point is there has to be a greater good that you are chasing, a higher purpose.

Lesson Three: *Build a network of developmental relationships.*

One of the keys to spiraling upward in any profession is mentoring. Not only do mentors provide advice and support; they can play a significant role in personal and professional development, particularly early in your career. A mentor can help you understand the formal and informal policies, procedures, and agendas at your company or organization. Must a mentor be someone you can "relate" to because they share your background or style? Not necessarily. None of the mentors who played significant roles in my life were Black men, though I frequently wished some of them were.

In my opinion, different kinds of mentors support different aspects of your development. So it is important to have several people in that role. It is also important to reassess these relationships periodically, as you will need different types of support at different points in your career. Early on, it is likely that your mentors will be people with whom you have regular contact—an employer, supervisor, or respected colleague. As you progress, you may seek out a trusted client or seasoned leader who has complimented your work. Even today, after a fifty-year career, I still have mentors with whom I consult on important matters.

How do you find a mentor? Not by waiting around for an invitation. Most mentors do not go hunting for mentees. You must seek them out, as I did with Aldo Parisot.

You must be proactive. Most importantly, you must present yourself in such a manner that potential mentors will be attracted to assisting you on your journey.

Lesson Four: *Race and gender matter, but they alone do not determine your fate.*

No one should be naive about the very real challenges that people of color and women face in the workplace. But that does not mean problems that appear to be race– or gender-oriented are unsolvable. My father's approach to the double consciousness that all Black people in America must cultivate was to insist that, while white people might not appreciate our beauty and brilliance, we should always walk with pride. In addition to being Black, we were Americans, he always said, entitled to exactly the same rights, privileges, and opportunities as the majority. In the United States, we are barely two generations beyond legal segregation by race. So, it shouldn't be surprising that most of our educational institutions still maintain practices that could be described as inherently racist. For instance, the intake practices of sororities and fraternities. But that does not mean I have outlawed these organizations at UR. It means that people of color must continue to share our perspectives.

It remains a burden to be Black in America. But Blacks must never allow race to be an excuse for abandoning our individual paths toward growth. I am a firm believer that you are who, and what, you think you are. If you buy into the messages promulgated by internalized racism (i.e. negative stereotypes), you will limit your potential. This is, in my opinion, the primary reason that Lesson One is so critically important.

Lesson Five: *Do not forget to take time for yourself and for your family.*

Despite the early battles I've described with my father, family has been an essential source of grounding and strength throughout my life. And, just like professional pursuits, a solid family demands work. My ancestry is part of my family too, of course, and every day that I walk into my office, I understand that I am standing on the shoulders of my forebearers. My father, as I've mentioned, became the first Black manager at the Cincinnati Milacron machine tool company, though he never finished high school. That I hold a doctorate from Yale University and serve as the first Black president of the University of Richmond are sources of pride to me every day.

You must always remember the relationship with your family, your partner, your mentors, and your closest friends. Schedule time for those people who matter most. Keep them in your life—even if only by text or Zoom or Instagram, even when it feels difficult. It is important. And remember to schedule time just for yourself, too.

Chapter Eleven:
STEPPING FORWARD

I'VE BUILT MUCH of my life and career around cultivating a public profile of restraint. During my own college days—despite being a conscientious objector to the Vietnam War and attending a march after Dr. King's assassination—I did not engage much with politics. There comes a time, however, when a man must step forward. I felt it in 1968, and I feel it again today.

Much of the social progress I've witnessed over the past fifty years—a growing appreciation for the benefits of diversity, and efforts to broaden circles of access—appears today to be crumbling. If there is anything about the Trump administration for which I am grateful, it is the way it ripped the curtain away and exposed these deep schisms in America. Most people understand that the hatred displayed nightly on newscasts has always existed; it is only now being displayed nakedly, without shame or fear, and it is forcing harsh conversations. For many students on our campuses, this is the first time they've openly confronted issues of race, religion, and gender. Indeed, many will be interacting with people who are different from them for the first time in their lives. The four years that they spend in college may be the last opportunity they have to learn how to have conversations across religious, racial, and ideological difference. This means that we, as campus administrators, have a brief window to make an important difference in the lives of our students and, by extension, the future of this country. So, despite rough moments and pain, we're going to keep talking and working toward a new understanding of ourselves. It won't be comfortable, and there will be missteps. But isn't that the purpose of a liberal arts education?

I have to give Betty credit for initially raising my consciousness with regard to stepping forward. Early in our marriage, when I was teaching at the University of North Carolina at Greensboro and she had started working as assistant to the chancellor, I was wrestling with a problem regarding an administrative decision with which I did not agree. "Stop complaining and do something about it!" she snapped at me one night. At the time, I was upset with her for being so direct. But I knew she was right. So, I got myself elected as a member-at-large to the University Senate.

This move changed many things for me. Though I'd engaged a bit in faculty governance before, I now became much more intentional about that work. And a lot more confident. For instance, after I'd been on the Senate a few years and had won tenure, I asked a colleague how one got elected to the University Promotion and Tenure Committee. You had to be nominated, she told me and then asked, "Would you like me to nominate you?" It was as simple as that. Being elected to the committee opened up a whole new world to me, provding an important and illuminating look at the mechanics and discussions behind every tenure decision in the university.

As the lone Black faculty member in the School of Music, I was very interested in the experience of Black people at the UNC–Greensboro and became an active member of the Black Faculty and Staff Association. Eventually, I was chosen to be its president. This brought me face to face with the Chancellor, who several times sought my opinion on issues related to cultural diversity. He asked me about unconscious bias in the faculty search process. Well, I told him, it wasn't all that unconscious. I'd seen candidate resumes tossed if they had graduated from HBCUs. He was incredulous, shocked that hiring committees at the school he led could be so narrow-minded.

I also pushed to diversify the curriculum in the School of Music. There was no Black music other than jazz covered in any of the required courses or electives, and only minimally at that. So, I developed a course in African-American Music for non-music majors. It was a hugely popular, and I enjoyed working with this broader range of students. However, I remained concerned about the fact that we were graduating music majors—many of whom would be teaching Black and brown students in the public schools—who knew so little about American music.

A colleague and I proposed a course for music majors called Music History: The American Scene. This was somewhat controversial at the time because the course lay far outside the canon of classical music history. But I felt strongly that we were doing our students a disservice by allowing them to graduate without any knowledge of American music, which included Black music. Though I was not yet tenured, I felt that I needed to take a forceful stand in support of this course during discussions among the music faculty, regardless of the consequences. It was a risk. But there are moments in all our lives when the cost of shrinking away is greater than the consequences of stepping forward. In this case, my course was narrowly approved by the music faculty. But if it had been rejected, and if that had tarnished my chances to earn tenure, I would not have wanted to remain on the faculty at UNC–Greensboro. To me, the matter was that important.

A few years after these negotiations, the University Senate at UNC decided to devote an entire meeting to cultural diversity on campus. It was the 1980s, when higher education was finally beginning to confront such issues, and as the president of the Black Faculty and Staff Association, as well as a member of the Senate, I was tapped to be one of the speakers. A sociology professor from an HBCU across town, North Carolina A&T University, was also invited to address the group, along with one of our Black students. I thought long and hard about what

I wanted to say. The status of Blacks at UNCG was not good, in my view. But I knew that airing this perspective might mean I'd never be promoted to full professor. I shared my concerns with Betty, and she agreed: it was more important to be honest.

I meditated and prayed a lot in the days leading up to the meeting. As I made my way to the front of the room and stood before the podium, my heart was pounding. I looked out at a crowd of mostly white faces, then took a deep breath and began my remarks. I congratulated Chancellor Moran for his leadership in overseeing the construction of several new buildings on campus, but, I added, bricks and mortar do not a university make. It is the people who create a university, and it was my belief that Black people were not thriving at UNCG. I was pleasantly surprised at the loud, enthusiastic applause that followed. With a sense of relief, I returned to my seat and attempted to keep my head down for the rest of the meeting.

When it concluded, I tried to leave quickly. But the vice chancellor for Academic Affairs stopped me. Her assistant had been trying to reach me for a week, she said. I braced myself for whatever boom might be lowered. "I want you to consider becoming a member of my team," the vice chancellor continued, as I doubled over with laughter and relief. The vice chancellor was a bit startled by the intensity of this reaction and asked if there was anything amiss. No, nothing at all, I said, with a smile.

However, when she and I sat down to discuss the position about a week later, it became clear that I was being pigeonholed into a "minority" slot. The vice chancellor said she wanted me to assist with recruiting faculty of color while overseeing the retention of students of color. I told her I was more interested in undergraduate studies and faculty development. Then came the salary discussions. I was making more money with private students and my position in the Greensboro Symphony than what she was offering. If I became a full-time administrator, I explained, I would have to resign from the symphony and probably give up teaching too. We came to an agreement over my pay and duties. I would serve for one year as acting assistant vice chancellor for Academic Affairs/Faculty Development and Undergraduate Instruction. But I would also assist with the recruitment of Black faculty.

On my first day with the new job, I sat at my broad desk and wrote myself a note:

1. Remember how you got here: by virtue of being an outstanding faculty member.
2. Remember why you are here: to serve.
3. Do not become obsessed with positional power.

Then I tucked the note into my new desk drawer.

A tool that became immensely useful to me in my new leadership role was re-evaluation counseling, sometimes called co-counseling. It's an approach to personal change based on reciprocal relationships. Each person takes a turn in the role of counselor and must give full attention to the other, who is talking. But this is not a discussion. The counselor's main purpose is to support the "client" in working through their own issues. Betty had been introduced to re-evaluation counseling by a history professor at UNCG, and I was skeptical as I listened to her describe what they did in class: namely, holding hands and listening very closely. The holding hands part in particular did not appeal to me. However, I could not help noting the positive impact it seemed to have on Betty, so eventually I decided to give it a try. This is where I began to understand the value of active listening, the skill that has been most important to me as a leader.

During my first year as interim assistant vice chancellor for Academic Affairs, I continued to teach cello. I had about ten students, and thought I could do it all. But it became increasingly difficult to give them the kind of attention they were accustomed to receiving (a fact that became painfully obvious when I was forced to take a call with a finalist for the position of library director in the midst of giving a cello lesson). But I liked being an administrator more than I'd anticipated. Every day I faced new challenges to be resolved, and when the university offered me a permanent position as associate vice chancellor, I took it. During my two years in that role, I logged several accomplishments, including the establishment of UNCG's first faculty development office; spearheading a plan for recruiting faculty of color; and assisting department chairs on faculty recruitment, promotion, and tenure.

I was shaping the culture of an institution, and this proved to be immensely gratifying. Still I yearned to be doing this at an arts school. The vice chancellor intimated that I would eventually step into the role of dean of the School of Music, and she encouraged me to discuss my promotion to full professor with the current dean. But when I sat down with him, I got a gut punch. The dean did not think my teaching warranted promotion to full professor, he said, because a student had complained after I told her that she could no longer be a music major. The young woman in question had studied with me as a high school student, and barely met the requirements to become a music major. I had warned her that without more consistent practice and improvement, she would be in danger of removal. But I did not argue with the dean. I simply scheduled another appointment. This time, I brought a champion with me, the head of instrumental music, who pointed out that my teaching evaluations had always been very good. "But not excellent," the dean said.

I wondered what was really behind this back-and-forth. The faculty handbook clearly stated that the standard for promotion to full professor was "good" teaching. Was the dean searching for a way to avoid confrontation with some other problem?

The vice chancellor suggested that I keep arguing my case, pointing out my worth. But I was done. I'd been nominated for several leadership positions in other institutions by then, and I accepted one as vice president for Academic Affairs and dean of the conservatory at the Cleveland Institute of Music, one of the finest music schools in the country. I won't pretend modesty here or hide the fact that it felt good to announce my appointment to the dean who'd looked down his nose at me.

One of my first official assignments was to lead the school's inaugural in-house strategic planning process. I'd had considerable experience doing this at UNCG, and felt confident about leading the process at the Cleveland Institute. But, again, I faced skepticism, this time about my ability to actively engage faculty in the process. Nonetheless, I was able to involve even those professors who were members of the Cleveland Orchestra—including John Mack, one of the world's greatest oboists, who met with me for hours each week. When I presented the strategic plan to CIM's board six months later at the historic Union Club downtown, they approved it on the spot. At the Cleveland Institute, I was once again the only Black administrator, and it soon became clear that the faculty were woefully ignorant about Black musicians and composers. To address this, I began planning a concert for Black History Month featuring all-Black pieces. It soon became an annual event.

Betty, Sara, and I loved living in Cleveland. We had a beautiful colonial home in Cleveland Heights that had been designed by Bloodgood Tuttle. Betty was appointed as the first director of community relations at the Cleveland Clinic Foundation. We were members of a terrific church, Mt. Zion Congregational, in University Circle, and we developed a strong circle of friends. Betty's father lived nearby. We thought we'd be there for many years.

However, all organizations breed a certain amount of office politics, and the Cleveland Institute was no different. When a new chairman of the board became increasingly displeased with CIM's president, he decided that I would step in as interim president. But he'd never informed me. I found out when a friend mentioned that he'd been contacted by someone from an executive search firm doing a background check into my leadership capabilities. From there, things only grew murkier.

The president, hearing of these backroom machinations, called me on a Sunday morning when I was visiting my aunt in New Haven, Connecticut, and accused me of undermining his leadership. Eventually the story of chaos and conspiracy at CIM leaked to Cleveland's newspaper *The Plain Dealer*, and I was summoned to appear before the faculty, along with several colleagues. I refused. I knew I'd done nothing wrong, and as the only Black member of the faculty or administration I was not going to allow myself to be humiliated. I simply declined to participate. When it became clear that reconciliation was impossible, I began looking for a new job.

One of my colleagues had nominated me for a position at the University of Texas at Austin, so I visited the campus. I was only going to learn more about the university's storied music program, I told Betty. There was no way we were moving to Texas! This is when I learned never say never. The University of Texas at Austin offered me a position as the first director of UT's School of Music. With almost a thousand students, the music program at

UT–Austin was one of the largest in the United States. Yet, from 1938 until the fall of 1994 when I arrived, music had been only a department in Fine Arts at UT, rather than designated as its own School. To those outside of academe, this may seem like a negligible distinction. I assure you, it is not. The difference is reflected in budget size, faculty draw, and prestige.

The long diminishment of music at UT–Austin was due mainly to a quirk of history. "Ma" Ferguson, who became the infamous governor of Texas after her husband was impeached and convicted, had scratched the university's original School of Music from the state budget in a petulant line-item veto during the 1930s. But in President Robert Berdahl, the music faculty finally had a leader who was receptive to rectifying this longstanding slight.

The dean of the College of Fine Arts, John Whitmore, was determined to appoint me as the new School of Music's first director, a thrilling prospect. But before accepting, I told him that I needed to visit Austin with my family. Could we really live in Texas, land of cowboys and cactuses? Betty and I had never thought of Texas as a terribly cultured place. But, again, test your assumptions. During our visit, we met numerous civic and cultural leaders, among them Bryce Jordan. As president emeritus of Penn State University, Jordan was revered among musicians nationwide as the first professional instrumentalist to serve as president of a large university. He'd previously chaired UT–Austin's Department of Music and had retired in Austin to serve as an advisor to the university's College of Fine Arts.

I consulted with several of my mentors and advisors before signing on, including Robert Freeman, the famed pianist, educator, and musicologist, who was then at the Eastman School of Music; Joe Polisi, president of the Juilliard School; and Robert J. Werner, a longtime music educator who was dean at the Cincinnati College Conservatory of Music. Each had known me for years and understood my heart as well as my goals. Each described the School of Music at UT–Austin as a "hidden gem" with tremendous potential. The only negative might be the music faculty: it had a reputation as one of the most cantankerous and difficult in the profession, my mentors said. During my second visit to Austin I decided to confront this possible problem head-on. I met with each of the departments in the music school, and told them what I'd heard. How did they feel about having such a reputation? I asked. Was it something they were proud of? Their responses, which ranged from surprise to regret, convinced me that I would have a core of colleagues willing to work with me in moving the school forward. I accepted the position.

Bryce Jordan turned out to be one of the most significant mentors in my life. He was the only person at UT who was aware that I'd had an opportunity to be considered for the dean's position at Yale, my alma mater. At my first Fine Arts Advisory Council meeting, which Bryce chaired, he mentioned to the group that I had bypassed this opportunity at Yale in favor of UT–Austin. This, of course, raised my stock in the eyes of the Texans. Bryce served as a critical connector between me and Austin's civic leaders. He and his wife hosted a reception for Betty and me in their home, where he made certain to introduce us to the city's cultural elite. Bryce and Elspeth Rostow, wife of Walt Rostow and the first dean of UT's LBJ School of Public Affairs, nominated me for membership in the Philosophical Society of Texas. Every prominent CEO and politician in Texas was a member of this prestigious organization, patterned after Benjamin Franklin's American Philosophical Society, Bryce told me; if nothing else, membership would be extremely helpful for fundraising purposes.

Bryce and his wife, Jonelle, had been involved in helping to recruit us to UT–Austin. When Betty, Sara, and I visited Austin to figure out whether we could actually envision living there, the Jordans invited us to a gala for the College of Fine Arts. Bryce made certain to introduce us to the movers and shakers in attendance. He also took time to explain why he felt becoming the first director of the School of Music at UT–Austin would be a good move for me. For this reason, it shouldn't have surprised me when, some years later, he quickly pivoted from a conversation about fundraising to the topic he really wanted to discuss: his aspirations for my career.

"It is obvious to me that you are going to become a university president," Bryce said. *What on earth had led him to that conclusion?* I thought, keeping mum. When he continued, asking what sort of university I envisioned leading, I quietly panicked. I had never seriously considered becoming a university president—how in the world could I answer his question about the kind of institution I should lead? All I knew was that I'd never show such uncertainty to someone who had so much faith in me. I tried to wing it, talking about the liberal arts. But I replayed the conversation on a loop in my head for days.

Following that lunch, Bryce began to nominate me for presidencies. My first interview was at Sarah Lawrence College in 1997. In advance, Bryce invited me to his home for a coaching session, during which he drilled me with questions that I might be asked by the search committee. At the end of our session, he asked what I thought of my chances. Very low, I told him. I had no illusions about getting the position at Sarah Lawrence, but I hoped to do well enough in the interview for the executive search firm to nominate me for other presidencies. A sensible way to approach the process, Bryce agreed, adding that he too had been "a bridesmaid" in several presidential searches. He listed them, one by one. When he got to the eighth, I was shaking my head in disbelief.

There is no doubt in my mind that my five years at UT–Austin prepared me to become a university president. It was an incredibly complex and political institution. All decisions had to be in accord with two tomes called the Regents' Rules. The leaders of every academic unit in the school spent inordinate amounts of time trying to circumvent the Regents' Rules. But Austin was also where I learned about the importance of marketing in raising a university's profile. Frankly, it wasn't all that difficult. The School of Music had two nationally-renowned composers so I began a Visiting Composers Series, reaching out to their network, and mine. We would feature two or three guest composers each year, and in this way we were able to bring some of the country's best to Austin for very low fees. The violinist Itzhak Perlman visited and performed the Tchaikovsky Violin Concerto with our student orchestra. Pretty soon, our program began to attract national buzz. Each composer stayed with us for a day or two, working with students who would perform their compositions. On top of this, I established a visiting committee of national leaders in music education, each one of whom spent two days at our school twice a year. Among them were the manager of the Cleveland Orchestra, two deans from the music schools at Oberlin and Yale, the head of the Aspen Music Festival, and the head of the Concert Artists Guild. I knew they would become ambassadors for UT, telling our story across the country.

During my last year at UT–Austin, I was the only internal candidate recommended to be the dean of Fine Arts. As it turned out, Bryce Jordan was the chair of the search committee. After the search consultants at Korn Ferry made their recommendation, Bryce asked if I knew of any reason why the head of the Performing Arts Center and the art museum would not want me in that job. Neither had supported my candidacy. I could think of nothing, I said, except that, as their colleague, I knew where all the bodies were buried. I wondered if UT–Austin was ready to have a Black dean of Fine Arts; at that point there had been only one Black dean in all of UT's history, and there were no other Blacks in senior leadership. "Do you really think the university is ready for a Black dean of Fine Arts?" I asked him point blank.

"I can't answer that," Bryce said. "But I know they're ready for a Dean Crutcher."

I appreciated his confidence. But within an hour of our conversation, I received a call from the president of Miami University informing me that I was his preferred candidate for the provost position there.

Chapter Twelve:
You Can Go Home Again

When I graduated from Miami University in 1969, I swore that I would never return. While I'd received an excellent education, my overall experience left a bitter taste. Certainly, Miami could have done more to help people of color feel included, but the primary cause of my discomfort at Miami was due to my own naivete. Despite weekly music lessons on campus throughout most of high school, I had been pretty clueless about college life. I am an introvert by nature, and while I've learned to disguise this over the years, as an eighteen-year-old freshman, I felt completely out of place in the party-as-much-as-you-can campus culture. My response was to sequester myself in study, which was good for my grades, but not so great for creating a sense of belonging.

Over the years, I'd received regular inquiries about coming back to Miami to teach. Initially, I was recruited to replace Liz Potteiger after she retired. Later, I was nominated to apply for head of the Music Department, dean of the School of Fine Arts, provost, and finally president. I declined every overture. I'd grown to like living in larger, more cosmopolitan cities. The idea of living in Oxford, Ohio, was not terribly attractive.

But life has a way of bringing us face-to-face with the things from which we run. In the spring of 1999, while I was at UT–Austin, my Aunt Jennie passed away. She was a nurse by training and had been caring for my mother, who was under treatment for multiple myeloma, for more than eight years. Aunt Jennie's death revealed a side to my mother that I'd never known. At the funeral, I saw her shed tears for the first time in my life. I decided then and there that I needed to find a way to get back to Ohio.

I had already been nominated for the presidency of Baldwin-Wallace University in Berea, Ohio, and my interviews seemed to go well. I had read all of the materials and prepared meticulously. At my finalist's interview, I presented an opening statement that touched on each of the sixteen criteria for president that the school's search committee had developed, and I left feeling very confident of my prospects. I was shocked to receive a call soon after, informing me that the committee had appointed someone else. I had "talked my way out of a job," the committee representative said.

What could that possibly mean? Frankly, said the man on the phone, my opening statement had intimidated the search committee. I'd been too aggressive, too prepared. I had covered everything they'd planned to ask about, leaving them no room to develop their own opinions. This was an important lesson for me, one of those "a-ha!" moments. As an academic, I had learned to do my home-work and offer exactly what I thought was expected. What I had failed to account for was the fact that, while all of the search committee members were all accomplished, they were primarily first-generation college graduates who might be easily put off by anyone who came on too force-fully. This perspective had never occurred to me, and it led me to a realization—or I should say, strategy—that has stayed with me since: don't lay all your cards on the table at once. Hold something back for later.

Soon after this disappointing phone call I had an oppor-tunity to put its lessons into action. Less than an hour after I received my rejection from Baldwin-Wallace, a friend who also happened to be an executive search consultant rang to ask if I could recommend anyone for a search he was doing on behalf of Miami University. Miami was looking for a new provost, and the search committee had not been impressed with the candidates they'd interviewed thus far. "Well, what about me?" I asked. "I'd be inter-ested in that position."

I flew to Cincinnati for my interview at Miami U during the last week of March 1999, two months after Aunt Jennie's funeral. This time, I was measured in my responses, careful to answer each question directly, but succinctly. At one point, I noticed the woman organiz-ing the search whisper to the committee chair. Then she stood and left the room. When she returned, there was more whispering, and the chair asked if I might have time to stop by the President's residence before returning to Cincinnati.

President James Garland welcomed me at the door and led me to a sun porch at the back of his spacious home. He was a clean-cut white man with dark hair and a pleasant smile. We spent almost an hour discussing leadership in higher education, liberal arts, the impact of grade inflation, and many other matters. He tended to angle his head and cast his eyes downward as he spoke, not because he was disengaged, but because he was, like me, an introvert. Still, I appreciated his style. I felt that I could be direct with him, even when disagreeing. It was clear, for instance, that he held rather negative views about the effectiveness of shared governance. (At Miami, the provost presided over the University Senate, and President Garland viewed this as a role that made the position less attractive to applicants.) Well, I was a champion of shared governance, I told him. In fact, I'd won my first position as an administrator because I'd been effective as a member of the Faculty Senate back at UNC–Greensboro fifteen years earlier. Despite our differences on the matter of shared governance, I came away from my chat with President Garland feeling that he and I could work together. In fact, I thought our strengths would complement one another.

Within a few days, President Garland phoned to inform me that I was his preferred candidate for the position. Now he wanted me to return with my family for a few days of more conversation and a meeting with the chair of the Board of Trustees. From the beginning of the search process, I'd been clear that my family and I would reside in Cincinnati. The thought of living in the small town of Oxford, thirty-five miles away, was not attractive to Betty. Also, my mother needed me in Cincinnati, and Sara, who'd spent much of her growing-up in Austin, was dead set against living in a provincial, Midwestern town. I pointed to my future colleague, Dr. Myrtis Powell, as an example. Dr. Powell, the vice president for Student Affairs, had become the first Black senior officer in Miami's history, and though she maintained an apartment on campus, Dr. Powell returned home to Cincinnati most nights.

But to my surprise, Dr. Powell insisted that I live in Oxford. Miami had burned through several provosts in the last ten years and the faculty were weary. My living in Oxford was imperative, Dr. Powell said. "If you don't, people will assume that you are just passing through like all of the others." Also, there were incalculable intelligence benefits to be gained simply by living, shopping, and supping in this small town. About that, she was absolutely correct.

Sara was furious and vowed never to forgive me. Part of the problem was her education. The local public schools were not a good fit for students with ADHD. But there was a special program at St. Ursula Academy, designed for girls of above-average intelligence who also had learning disabilities. We toured St. Ursula's on Memorial Day. Halfway through the visit, Sara looked at me with a smile and nodded approvingly.

Still, living in Oxford upended our household routines. In Austin, Sara took the school bus every day. In Oxford, Betty had to drive her thirty-seven miles each way. (Eventually, we met a family who lived between the school and our home, so Betty only had to drive half of the distance.) And reluctant as I had been to return to Miami, coming back as an accomplished alumnus to serve as provost and executive vice president gave me quite a bit of political capital. I look back at some of the decisions I made during my first year and wonder if I could have survived them as an outsider. At my first Provost's Breakfast of academic deans and department heads, I launched in: We think we're pretty good, here at Miami, I said. But what do we base that on? Where's the evidence?

My question was intentionally provocative. For years, Miami had been recognized as the "Public Ivy of Ohio." But I'd learned during the search process that Miami's honors program, of which I was a graduate, was not considered by students to be as competitive as that at Ohio State, nor even the honors program at Kent State. For the first time in Miami's history, more students who had applied to both Miami and Ohio State were matriculating at the latter. This was unheard of! But there were clear reasons. While some schools would use the "public Ivy" reputation as permission to be even more exclusive, Miami had moved in the opposite direction, recruiting well-rounded B+ students, as opposed to aiming only for straight-A types.

There is no such thing as stasis for an academic institution. I told the school's leaders that if we were not constantly assessing and refining the quality of our academic offerings and research, we would fall behind. At another breakfast, I introduced the concept of benchmarking against other universities, asking each school and academic department to identify three to five peer programs and others to which they aspired. This request provoked more than a bit of controversy. Most of Miami's department chairs had no idea how to go about benchmarking. One opined that his department had no aspirational peers—no other institution in the country prepared students as well as they did! I could see that some education would be necessary for these educators.

Still more controversial was my decision to cut Miami's nursing program from the Oxford campus. It had been initially introduced as a completion program located on regional campuses. Nurses who were already LPNs could take the coursework and exams necessary for a bachelor's degree and certification. But over the years this program had migrated onto the Oxford campus. We'd considered founding a School of Allied Health Sciences, and nursing would have been part of it. But when it became clear that such a school was not feasible, I decided to close nursing on our Oxford campus.

This naturally provoked tremendous outcry from nursing students and faculty. Throughout the spring of 2000, signs cropped up across the campus encouraging people to contact my office and decry my decision. Yet I did not receive a single note asking me to reconsider. The hardest part was explaining all of this to our students. I'd count it among the five most difficult conversations I've had as a professional. I didn't have the heart to tell them that nursing was never envisioned as part of the Oxford campus; that felt like rubbing salt on an open wound. So, I just listened as these students expressed their disillusionment. There have been few times in my life when I felt as demoralized. Betty reminded me not to take any of it personally, which is exactly what I was doing. This is an important point that I share with all of my mentees—very few reactions are motivated by personal antipathy—but in this situation I had to be reminded of that. As I've said, remaining centered and listening actively are skills that require constant practice, just like playing an instrument.

Five years at Miami, combined with my experiences at UT–Austin, prepared me to become a college president. Yet this goal continued to elude me. I was a runner-up at several more institutions, and grew quite frustrated. Maybe a college presidency wasn't in the cards for me after all, I thought. In the meantime, I reconnected with my parents. Every Saturday morning, I drove to College Hill, a suburb of Cincinnati, to get my hair trimmed. Afterward, I visited with my mother while my father went to make sandwiches for the less fortunate at Zion Baptist Church. Though my mother was less active in the congregation, she'd been a woman of deep faith all her life. By this point, she had been suffering with multiple myeloma for several years, and I'd accompany her to chemotherapy sessions. I was with her in the final hour, my first experience seeing life pass out of a person, and afterward I read though her diaries. Only then did I realize how important faith had been in sustaining her through an eleven-year battle with cancer. I feel blessed to have been there for most of it.

None of this would have happened had I not taken advantage of a fortuitous telephone inquiry to nominate myself for the position of provost. What I learned from the Miami experience is to never say "never." For years I'd been adamant about not returning to the school where I'd been an undergraduate. But Miami became foundational to my growth and development. It allowed me to be with my mother at the end of her life. It taught me that it is indeed possible to go home again, to walk the same ground I had so many years before, and to spiral higher.

Chapter Thirteen:
COMING FULL CIRCLE

WHEN I STEPPED down as president of Wheaton College after ten years, it was my intention to return to the performing arts field in some manner. While several mentors urged me not to make any decisions about next steps for at least six months, I acted against their advice when an executive search firm consultant called to tell me about an opening for presidency of the Chicago Symphony Orchestra. This intrigued me, especially since Sara was then living in Chicago. At least I'd have the opportunity to take her out to dinner now and then. I agreed to interview for the position.

But halfway through the interview, it became clear that I did not have much passion for this role. I was trying to respond to a question about the importance of educational programming for the symphony, and an inner voice fairly shouted, *You don't really want this job!* It startled me, frankly, and made it almost impossible for me to continue the conversation. Somehow I got through the interview. But immediately afterward, I wrote the search consultant a note declining to go any further with the process. "It's probably best for me to stay in my own lane," I said. What I meant was that I'd realized it was best for me to stay with what I knew and loved best: higher education.

Meanwhile, Betty and I were leaving the Northeast for a ten-month sabbatical in Berlin. While there, I reflected. Being president of Wheaton from 2004 to 2014—arguably ten of the most challenging years for anyone to lead a tuition-dependent liberal arts college—had shown me just how much I loved the liberal arts. Despite its many challenges, the time at Wheaton had flown. I told Betty that if I could find another small college or university whose faculty and staff took their roles as mentors as seriously as Wheaton faculty and staff, I would take on another presidency.

I responded to executive search inquiries only if I felt the institution was a good fit. By the time a consultant for the University of Richmond contacted me, I was a finalist for the presidency of a school in the Western US. But the Richmond consultant did not give up easily. She asked me to get in touch after I'd visited that other campus. Well, ok, I thought. And as Betty and I were walking out of our Berlin apartment to go to the airport for my interview, I grabbed the Richmond prospectus on a whim. If nothing else, it would give me something to read on our flight.

The longer I studied the Richmond prospectus, the more interesting the university became to me. Not least, because it was located in the South, in a city that once had been the capital of the Confederacy. Also, the campus was beautiful. Most of the buildings were designed in the collegiate gothic style developed by Ralph Adams Cram (who'd also done Wheaton's campus, as well as Princeton's, Rice's, Sweet Briar's, Wellesley's, and many others). But what intrigued me more than Richmond's location and beauty was the energy UR had put toward diversity—and how much progress the university had made in less than ten years. After the rocky encounters around true inclusion at Wheaton, I was eager to see how another campus had handled the same challenge.

The coordinate college system also interested me. While Richmond is fully cocducational, there still exist vestiges of its old single-sex system, with one dean for the male-oriented Richmond College and another for Westhampton College, which had eduated young women. Today, this approach provides female students an equal opportunity for leadership in governance because each college has its own student association. My own daughter had also benefited from her experience at a single-sex high school, so I believed in the value of focusing on particular types of students as a cohort. The final, critical factor was Richmond's need-blind admissions policy: the school provided 100% of demonstrated need to all qualified students. Financial aid had been the aspect of my tenure at Wheaton that rankled most. At least once a year, I'd hear from a parent or high school counselor wondering why a talented student had been placed on the Wait List. I could never reveal the true reason students weren't readily accepted: too many tuition loans. By the time Betty and I were flying over the Atlantic, I knew Richmond's need-blind admissions policy made it the right fit for me. The moment we landed, I called the search consultant and told her that I wanted to be a candidate.

A little more than a month later, I was once again flying from Berlin to the US, this time to meet with the UR search committee in Washington, DC. The day after my interview, the search consultant told me I was their unanimous choice, and that I should plan to return for a secret visit to the campus later that month. I was pleased with this news, of course, but somewhat taken aback. Had I been the only "finalist"? I asked. You are the "preferred finalist," she said, meaning that they would turn to the next candidate only if I turned them down.

After that, the process moved very fast. I met with some trustees in New York, had a telephone conversation with the rector summarizing their offer, and the next morning a breakfast with a search consultant who told me that I would have an offer in writing by the end of the week. Less than a month after my first interview, I was looking at a university presidency. It was a bit overwhelming. The day UR sent my official offer, Betty and I had planned to attend a performance of the singer Lionel Richie. He and Betty had grown up together in Tuskegee, and remained friends through the years. After the concert, we had dinner together and, bursting with excitement, I shared my big news.

My official introduction to the faculty and students was a boisterous event. Sara joined Betty and me on campus, where hundreds of people were assembled in the Robins Center, Richmond's basketball arena. The student government leaders presented us with UR sweatshirts, the young woman handing me a red one, and the young man giving Betty the blue, in recognition of the colleges' respective colors. Without missing a beat, Betty switched them, taking the red sweatshirt from me and handing over the blue one. That got people's attention!

Ron, Betty and Sara

For the next few hours, we met with members of the UR community. But among all the notables who spoke to me, I knew I wouldn't forget Dr. Tinina Cade. As associate vice president for student development, she had for many years been UR's only Black administrator, and she introduced me to Barry Greene, the first Black student to live on campus. In many ways, Greene and I had walked similar paths; while he was fighting for residency at UR in 1968, I was an undergraduate at Miami U, trying to figure out my own place in America's conversation around race. At the UR rally, I congratulated Greene for being a trailblazer, and said I hoped we might have a conversation about his experiences as a student.

In the summer of 2018, the two of us finally had that talk. We met in my nicely appointed office in the President's residence, and the hours flew by. Greene is a reserved man, quiet and somewhat old-fashioned. Despite living the history of desegregation in education, he is the farthest thing from a firebrand, so it was difficult for him to talk about those years when white students refused to sit with him in the dining hall and professors sometimes questioned if he was "in the right place" when they saw him sitting in the front of their classrooms. He'd enrolled at Richmond in the fall of 1968, and graduated in 1972. For the next forty years, he did not set foot on campus again. (Though Greene was the first Black student to reside on campus, there were two other Black students, Madieth Malone and Isabelle LeSane, both of whom lived at home and commuted to the university.)

As he spoke, it became clear that Greene was struggling to come to terms with today's reality, where many students of color insisted not on inclusion but instead on designated "safe spaces" and exclusionary organizations. "Why would you want to attend a predominantly white institution only to segregate yourself?" he kept asking. He couldn't get his head around it. Several months after our conversation, the university celebrated its fiftieth anniversary of Black student presence on campus. During meetings to organize that event, our Black alumni, including Mr. Greene, Ms. Malone, and Ms. LeSane, all now in their sixties, sat in amazement as today's students bitterly described how little life at UR had changed. I have rarely seen the generation gap displayed so clearly: our students were frustrated at the slow pace of change, yet here they were, speaking honestly about race from within the seat of the Confederacy, at a university led by a Black president.

During the anniversary celebration, I announced a Presidential Commission for University History and Identity, which would study UR's history and its implications for our current campus climate and future. I wanted them to:

- Explore how our institutional history had been recorded, preserved, and made accessible to a range of audiences;

- Re-examine our past to identify people and narratives previously excluded from our institutional history;

- And recommend ways to acknowledge and communicate that history inclusively.

It is difficult to convey just how revolutionary this was. As an institution founded to educate white men, located in the former capitol of the Confederacy, the University of Richmond has made enormous strides. But it is telling that we are only now beginning to lift up the stories of those enslaved people who worked on and inhabited our land. For instance, I'd long heard tell of a slave cemetery located on campus. But no one seemed to know anything about it. The President's Commission began research to identify its location, and discovered that builders had plowed a road straight through the site, twice relocating human remains. They also uncovered stories of several slaves who had worked and lived on this land. We erected a temporary memorial to identify the approximate location of the slave burial ground, and are planning a more permanent marker. Meanwhile, in a letter to the UR community and an op-ed in the local newspaper, university officials formally apologized.

We cannot rewrite the history of the University of Richmond, much less the Confederacy. But I believe that coming full circle to investigate and interrogate our past will contribute to making us a better, more inclusive community—on campus and beyond.

Coda: An Ear for Leadership

THERE ARE INFINITE ways to interpret a life. When I look back on mine, I realize how fortunate I've been. *Why me?* I often wonder. I did not begin my career as a cellist and music professor with any intention of shaping higher education for thousands of other students. As the Black son of working-class parents and the first person in my family to attend college, the inspiration for considering a career in higher education came from my first true mentor, Professor Elizabeth Potteiger, whose invitation to study cello for free quite literally changed my life. It exposed me to the world of college campuses, and presented career possibilities I had never even dreamed of. I think of Liz's impact daily, marveling at what might have become of me if we'd never met.

But there are other ways to see my story. Early on, I felt drawn to music, then cello, and I never ignored that pull. Indeed, I chased it. Professor Potteiger later said she was drawn to my musicality, the way I'd interpreted Bach that day she first saw me at the student competition in Oxford. But there were other talented young players there. Why did she approach me? And what led her to offer lessons for free? Was I part of Liz Potteiger's personal affirmative action plan, or was it something about my musicianship? Whatever her motivations, I see now how those early lessons with Liz laid the groundwork for my own leadership style—quiet, but exacting; disciplined but broad-minded.

Beyond mentors, none of us can discount the powerful influence of family. The circumstances of my childhood played a major role in shaping my character. Although I grew up self-conscious about my family's humble means and my father's working-class manners, I realize now how rich we were in other ways. I knew I was loved unconditionally, and that I would be safe in my home. We all know how many children cannot say this, and what frequently happens in their later lives. And by watching my father interact with our neighbors, most of them Jewish widows, I learned very early that differences in race and religion need not be a barrier to developing relationships. Most of all I learned from my dad how to remain optimistic—to see a glass half-full rather than almost drained, and how to be incessantly curious about everything. My mother was more of an introvert, and from her I learned to be aware, always, of how I present myself.

If I have any modicum of emotional intelligence, it is because of the impact of these three people. Hence, my approach to leadership involves body, mind, and soul, just like my approach to playing the cello.

Liz Potteiger taught me that the relationship of my body to the cello was like that of an athlete to their sport. Likewise, in leadership I believe it is critically important to remain in good physical shape. The endorphins released through exercise ensure an alert mind ready to solve challenges. Without regular physical activity, any leader risks overwhelm and, ultimately, poor performance.

I've mentioned the "S" shield I use to remind me always to think before acting. But there is another important way in which the mind can be used, particularly when dealing with difficult people. From my mother I learned that there is good in everyone. I later understood that most difficult people have been hurt by something early in their lives. The situation surrounding that hurt is lodged indelibly in their brains and often shapes their interactions with others, particularly under stress. When I encounter difficult people, I try to see through their hurt to the good person lodged behind it. This approach has been enormously helpful.

Finally, the soul or spirit must never be overlooked. I try to follow Matthew 5:16 "...let your light so shine that men will see your good works and glorify your Father who is in heaven." Meaning that every day I try to interact with colleagues in such a way that they can see the spirit within me.

As a leader, those who work with you want to know that you care about them. They crave evidence that you appreciate their efforts. Early in my career, this aspect of leadership was difficult for me. I am a no-nonsense type, and I used to proceed from the belief that people should just be quiet and do their jobs. I have mellowed considerably. A leader must be demonstrative—especially toward colleagues on the lower rungs. Among many wise things that I heard from Maya Angelou, one quote has remained front-of-mind: "People will forget what you said, people will forget what you did, but they will never forget how you made them feel."

I have not tried to present my leadership style as the perfect model for all to follow. My story is but one example of how to live a fulfilling and useful life. But even for those who choose alternative routes, there are three key principles that I would commend to anyone contemplating leadership—of whatever kind:

1. Know yourself.
2. Be kind to others, no matter how difficult they are.
3. Take care of yourself mentally and physically.

To know yourself is to know what you stand for. Leadership positions will test these values daily, sometimes to the breaking point. You must keep a steady eye on what is, and is not, acceptable to you. This may mean putting a stop to unethical practices; it may require courage or result in isolation. Those are the times that a personal moral compass will help.

Being kind to others no matter how difficult they are is a skill I have honed over many years. Early in my career, I simply blocked out troublesome people, as I'd once done to my dad. I tried to imagine they did not exist. I avoided them when I could, and if I could not, I interacted with them only in the most impersonal ways. Not a great strategy. Over the years I've learned that you will sometimes need to rely on difficult personalities, and even the most challenging person eventually responds to kindness.

Taking care of yourself mentally and physically is essential if one wants to thrive in stressful leadership positions. In Chapter Nine I outlined several ways to do this. I would add here that it is also important not to take oneself too seriously, and not to take criticism personally—whatever its source.

I hope you have found something in this book that is useful to you personally and professionally. I have not written it to demonstrate a model life. However, I have written it as an example of a life well-lived. A life that has transcended the potential obstacles of race and class. I leave you with one of my favorite quotes from Georgia O'Keeffe: "I have been terrified every day of my life, but that has never stopped me from doing anything that I wanted to do."

Acknowledgments

I BEGAN WRITING this memoir in the summer of 2013, as I prepared for a sabbatical in Berlin, Germany, following ten years as president of Wheaton College in Massachusetts. This was the first sabbatical of my entire academic career, and I'd planned to complete the manuscript during that time. However, upon arrival in Berlin I realized I was exhausted and that time spent reconnecting with myself, taking in all that this amazing city had to offer, was at that moment more important. Many memoirists have discovered the same: there are moments when it is important to gestate in one's impressions and memories and let life reshape them as it will. Taking this extra time turned out to be one of the most important decisions of my career. I would not have had the energy for another college presidency had it not been for those six months of respite.

It was Greg Shaw, a University of Richmond parent and the founder of Clyde Hill Publishing, who encouraged me to return to this project after I arrived at UR in 2015. After reading the few chapters I'd written in

Berlin, he asked if I would allow Clyde Hill to publish my book. For that I am eternally grateful. Greg understood what I wanted this work to be—both a memoir and meditation on leading across divides. The staff at Clyde Hill have been equally helpful. In particular, Claudia Rowe, who questioned, pushed, and cajoled me to uncover stories and perspectives that I had not considered in years. She helped me to understand the importance of turning experiences into story, helping readers visualize the moments that have formed my approach to life and leadership.

A handful of people deserve thanks for reading all or parts of the manuscript over the years it came together. Donna Heiland, who read the initial four chapters while I was still in Berlin, offered insight and encouragement. I also recognize Melody Barnes, Roger Brown, Aaron Dworkin, Freeman Hrabowski, and Ted Mitchell for taking time to review the manuscript and write brief testimonials. A special word of appreciation, too, to my dear friend and birthday sister Charlayne Hunter-Gault, for writing the foreword.

This memoir would not have been possible without the unconditional love of my parents, Andrew and Burdella Miller Crutcher. The work ethic and values they instilled in me made it possible to live a life worth writing about. I also would be remiss if I did not thank my mother's only surviving sister, Olivia Miller Yarbrough, who will be ninety-seven in 2021. Aunt Olivia, who has a mind like a steel trap, enriched this memoir enormously. In

Acknowledgments

particular, she provided valuable information about my parents' courtship. Finally, to Betty and Sara, thank you for your love, patience, and understanding. Without you, this book never would have been completed.